FreeBSD Mastery: ZFS

"Once again, a great FreeBSD book to read." — *Wendy Michele, nixCraft*

"ZFS Mastery covers what everyone using or administering these filesystems needs to know to work with them every day. It's fascinating to see how the system is used, having seen how it is implemented." — *George V. Neville-Neil, co-author of "Design and Implementation of the FreeBSD Operating System"*

Networking for Systems Administrators

"There is a lot of useful information packed into this book. I recommend it!" — *Sunday Morning Linux Review, episode 145*

After reading this book, you'll have a strong footing in networking. Lucas explains concepts in practical ways; he makes sure to teach tools in both Unix/Linux and Windows; and he gives you the terms you'll use to explain what you're seeing to the network folks. Along the way there's a lot of hard-won knowledge sprinkled throughout…" — *Slashdot*

FreeBSD Mastery: Specialty Filesystems

"a joy and treasure to read" — *Vivek Gite, nixCraft*

"I'm a fan of his books… he presents them in a way that makes them much more understandable. He has the right mix of humor and information." — *Sunday Morning Linux Review*

SSH Mastery

"…one of those technical books that you wouldn't keep on your bookshelf. It's one of the books that will have its bindings bent, and many pages bookmarked sitting near the keyboard." — *Steven K Hicks, SKH:TEC*

"…SSH Mastery is a title that Unix users and system administrators like myself will want to keep within reach…" — *Peter Hansteen, author of The Book of PF*

"This stripping-down of the usual tech-book explanations gives it the immediacy of extended documentation on the Internet. Not the multipage how-to articles used as vehicles for advertising, but an in-depth presentation from someone who used OpenSSH to do a number of things, and paid attention while doing it." — *DragonFlyBSD Digest*

Network Flow Analysis

"Combining a great writing style with lots of technical info, this book provides a learning experience that's both fun and interesting. Not too many technical books can claim that." — *;login: Magazine, October 2010*

"This book is worth its weight in gold." — *Utahcon.com*

"The book is a comparatively quick read and will come in handy when troubleshooting and analyzing network problems." —*Dr. Dobbs*

"Network Flow Analysis is a pick for any library strong in network administration and data management. It's the first to show system administrators how to assess, analyze and debut a network using flow analysis, and comes from one of the best technical writers in the networking and security environments." — *Midwest Book Review*

FreeBSD Mastery: Storage Essentials

"If you're a FreeBSD (or Linux, or Unix) sysadmin, then you need this book; it has a lot of hard-won knowledge, and will save your butt more than you'll be comfortable admitting. If you've read anything else by Lucas, you also know we need him writing more books. Do the right thing and buy this now." — *Slashdot*

"There's plenty of coverage of GEOM, GELI, GDBE, and the other technologies specific to FreeBSD. I for one did not know how GEOM worked, with its consumer/producer model – and I imagine it's complex to dive into when you've got a broken machine next to you. If you are administering FreeBSD systems, especially ones that deal with dedicated storage, you will find this useful." — *DragonFlyBSD Digest*

Absolute FreeBSD, 2nd Edition

"I am happy to say that Michael Lucas is probably the best system administration author I've read. I am amazed that he can communicate top-notch content with a sense of humor, while not offending the reader or sounding stupid. When was the last time you could physically feel yourself getting smarter while reading a book? If you are a beginning to average FreeBSD user, Absolute FreeBSD 2nd Ed (AF2E) will deliver that sensation in spades. Even more advanced users will find plenty to enjoy." — *Richard Bejtlich, CSO, MANDIANT, and TaoSecurity blogger*

"Master practitioner Lucas organizes features and functions to make sense in the development environment, and so provides aid and comfort to new users, novices, and those with significant experience alike." — *SciTech Book News*

"Absolute OpenBSD by Michael Lucas is a broad and mostly gentle introduction into the world of the OpenBSD operating system. It is sufficiently complete and deep to give someone new to OpenBSD a solid footing for doing real work and the mental tools for further exploration… The potentially boring topic of systems administration is made very readable and even fun by the light tone that Lucas uses."
— *Chris Palmer, President, San Francisco OpenBSD Users Group*

PGP & GPG

"…The World's first user-friendly book on email privacy…unless you're a cryptographer, or never use email, you should read this book." — *Len Sassaman, CodeCon Founder*

"An excellent book that shows the end-user in an easy to read and often entertaining style just about everything they need to know to effectively and properly use PGP and OpenPGP." — *Slashdot*

"PGP & GPG is another excellent book by Michael Lucas. I thoroughly enjoyed his other books due to their content and style. PGP & GPG continues in this fine tradition. If you are trying to learn how to use PGP or GPG, or at least want to ensure you are using them properly, read PGP & GPG." — *TaoSecurity*

Tarsnap Mastery

"If you use any nix-type system, and need offsite backups, then you need Tarsnap. If you want to use Tarsnap efficiently, you need Tarsnap Mastery." –*Sunday Morning Linux Review episode 148*

"This book is a great way to feel confident about backing up your data securely in cloud or through off-site backups, without compromising security or burning your pocket with enterprise grade products from IT vendors." — *Wendy Michele, nixCraft*

PAM Mastery

Michael W Lucas

Tilted
Windmill
Press

PAM Mastery

Author: Michael W Lucas
Copyediting: Lindy Lou Losh
Cover art: *Sysadmin Gothic*, by Eddie Sharam, after Grant Wood's *American Gothic*

ISBN-13: 978-1-64235-007-4
ISBN-10: 1-64235-007-9

Tilted Windmill Press
https://www.tiltedwindmillpress.com

PAM Mastery

Michael W Lucas

Brief Contents

Complete Contents

Acknowledgements

As always, I need to thank the technical reviewers who offered feedback on earlier drafts of this book: Bryan Irvine, Kurt Mosiejczuk, Mike O'Connor, and Carsten Strotmann. Special thanks go to Dag-Erling Smørgrav—the one-man army responsible for OpenPAM—who took time out of his busy schedule to educate me on some PAM fundamentals.

I also need to thank my horde of Twitter followers, who run many more operating systems than I believed were still in use, and cheerfully offered their particularly horrible PAM configurations for my edification.

All testing and research was done on servers from the generous folks at iX Systems, who have offered their support for my work for the last decade or so. The least I can do is thank them too.

Finally I'd like to thank the world, for letting me pretend that rsh(1), pam_rhosts, and their surrounding ecosystem do not exist.

For Liz.

Chapter 0: Introduction

Authentication on Unix-like systems is perhaps the closest thing sysadmins have to black magic.

Every sysadmin has heard of *Pluggable Authentication Modules,* or PAM. We all know that the files in `/etc/pam.d/` dictate how most software authenticates. If you want to use public key authentication, or authenticate with physical tokens, or rely only on passwords, you have to muck around in those files. Usually, sysadmins blindly follow the instructions and hope nothing terrible happens.

PAM policies are not exactly like anything else in systems administration. A set of PAM statements isn't processed like a set of packet filter rules or a shared library path, except when it is. Plus, PAM uses strange words like "requisite," and the word "sufficient" apparently means anything *but* "enough."

And when you break PAM, you break a whole service. Most services are hard enough to get running in the first place, so breaking them is discouraged. Hopefully it's not the service that lets you log in to the machine.

PAM doesn't have to be black magic, however. Enabling Google Authenticator doesn't absolutely *require* sacrificing a black cockerel on the thirteenth full moon of the year with a knife freshly forged from matrilineally inherited silver. All you need are your sysadmin skills and this book.

Prerequisites and Results

PAM Mastery is written for systems administrators of moderate experience. You need to understand managing shared libraries, installing and removing software, and troubleshooting your preferred platforms.

Not all platforms have packages for all of the modules discussed. Using these modules requires building them from source code. While I'll give basic instructions on compiling modules, those instructions assume that you've compiled software before and understand how your platform's compiler behaves. On CentOS, you'll need the "Development Tools" package group and the pam-devel package. On Debian you'll need the build-essentials and libpam0g-dev packages. The FreeBSD ports system contains all of the modules this book discusses.

This book focuses on cross-platform solutions, especially for educational purposes. Perhaps your Unix-like system has a PAM module for exactly a specific task. I'll occasionally mention such modules as we go, but pay most attention to modules used by multiple operating systems.

You'll also need systems to test on. The nice thing about experimenting with PAM is that system requirements are minimal. Virtual machines are perfectly suitable for testing PAM. If you're trying something like using pam_exec to spawn a Perl process to manage authentication, you'll want to perform load testing before deploying in production.

What will you get out of all of this? This book won't teach you the in-depth details of PAM on your preferred platform. It *will* teach you how to think about PAM, how the policies and modules work, and how to explore and master your preferred operating system's PAM implementation. You'll also carry the expertise gained here to any other PAM-using operating system.

What is Authentication?

Various security and computing bodies have redefined "authentication" to best suit their own needs. If you dig into security theory, you'll stumble across the term *Authentication, Authorization, and Accounting (AAA)*. Management Information Systems documents might focus on resource control, while sysadmins only care about matching the username and the password.

For purposes of PAM, *authentication* means validating a user's credentials and establishing service for people who provide those credentials. The security experts who use the AAA terminology will tell you that PAM pulls all those roles together. Which it does. PAM also lets you configure different modules and services for the various components of AAA, however.

PAM not only verifies authentication credentials. It can arrange home directories, log access, enable services, and more. PAM integrates system services with authentication.

If you're accustomed to the term *Identification, Authentication, and Authorization (IAA)*, you should know that PAM does not handle identification. Systems that rely on PAM normally use Name Service Switch (NSS) to manage identification. NSS also originated with Solaris, and predates PAM by a few years. The lack of integration between NSS and PAM has caused a continuous migraine for Unix-like systems ever since.

Multi-Factor Authentication

The phrase *two-factor authentication* gets batted around quite a bit. You can use PAM to implement two-factor authentication or, indeed, multi-factor authentication. The obvious question becomes: what is an authentication factor?

Authentication is based on one of three user characteristics: something they *have*, something they *know*, or something they *are*. "Something they have" refers to a physical token, such as a hardware security token or a cell phone tied to a specific phone number. These physical items are easily lost or broken. "Something they know" is a secret, such as a password—and we all know that passwords get written on sticky notes and attached to the monitor. "Something they are"— including biometric factors such as a fingerprint, an iris scan, or a gene scan—might seem best. But biometric data can be stolen. Changing your iris scan pattern in response to that theft is beyond the scope of this book.

Multi-factor authentication requires two or more of these factors. Maybe you need a security token and a particular cellphone and a password and a fingerprint. An intruder can capture any one of these without too much trouble, but grabbing every necessary piece is exponentially more difficult.

The second half of this book includes several PAM modules that add an authentication factor, such as Google Authenticator (Chapter 9) or used for specific purposes, like the pam_passwdqc password quality checker (Chapter 11).

Why PAM?

If Pluggable Authentication Modules are such a pain, why use them?

Because most of the alternatives are worse.

In the early days of computing, every program needed separate configuration to support any desired authentication methods. If you wanted a new workstation to match the standards demanded by your enterprise network, you needed to adjust every program on that workstation. Some of those programs needed configuration file changes, while others demanded full-out recompiling. No software or operating system supported all authentication methods. And if you wanted to do something even a little different… good luck!

Chapter 0: Introduction

In 1995, Sun Microsystems proposed a standard cross-platform, cross-program authentication interface. Software adopting this interface could utilize any authentication program offering that interface. If you wanted a new authentication mechanism for such programs, you could write it to attach to this interface and just plug it in to all your software. Hence, Pluggable Authentication Modules, or PAM.

PAM modules are chunks of code that implement a specific authentication method. You want to provide authentication with a username and password? That's a module. Via a hardware token? That's a module. Via gene scans, breathalyzer test, and a Dance Dance Revolution platform? Those would all be modules, too, if such things existed. (In an effort to be platform-agnostic, this book uses those three modules in many examples.[1]) Modules are shared libraries, dynamically linked into the main program as configured. Yes, the phrase "PAM module" is redundant, but that's what sysadmins call them, and I already have too many battles to fight to take this on.

Software that uses PAM receives authentication requests. The program hands each request off to the configured authentication modules, which tell the server if it should allow the authentication request or not.

Today, PAM is the most widely used authentication standard for Unix-like systems. It's overwhelmingly popular in the Linux world, as well as Solaris-based and BSD systems. Even Apple's OS X uses PAM, as well as commercial UNIX systems like AIX and HP-UX.

---

1   I wanted to use pam_hipster.so as a sample module, but it requires an artisan compiler that runs only on this one *fascinating* architecture. Plus, the code is only available via punch cards from this one guy who works at the custom bicycle shop down the road.

Strictly speaking, PAM is not an officially accepted standard. No Grand Certifying Body has placed its stamp on a set of PAM definitions and protocols and declared them the One True PAM Specification. The Common Desktop Environment (CDE) included PAM, and CDE became a standard back in the 1990s, so PAM does get referenced in various standards documents. Most modern PAM implementations are based on a draft specification from an attempt in 1997 to include PAM in the Portable Operating System Interface (POSIX). If you really want to dive into PAM, check out the document *X/Open Single Sign-on Service (XSSO) – Pluggable Authentication Modules*, available from a whole bunch of Internet sites, including http://pubs.opengroup.org. People have tried to standardize PAM since then, but all attempts have failed.

The absence of a formal standard means that PAM also lacks a formally defined language. Depending on which documentation you read, a group of rules might be a *chain* or a *stack* or a *policy*. A component of the authentication process might be a *type* or a *facility* or a *whatsit*. In this book I give the most common terms for each component, then choose a single word to be used for that component. The fact that I use a specific word to refer to a part of PAM doesn't mean that all the other choices are invalid; it only means that you lot need consistency if you're to understand this gobbledygook.

PAM Limitations

PAM is the most widely used authentication system, but its limitations make it unsuitable for some applications.

The biggest drawback to PAM is that a PAM module can't interact directly with clients. The server program is an intermediary between the PAM module and the client, and any interaction between the module and client is limited to that offered by the standard PAM interface.

Some authentication protocols, like Kerberos, include a whole sweeping array of client-server interactions that far exceed what PAM can support. In Kerberos, PAM is a bottleneck. While you can use PAM modules to support Kerberos, you cannot implement Kerberos through PAM. This is also why SSH handles most of its authentication outside PAM (although it can leverage PAM if you decide so).

This limitation is why people created other authentication protocols, such as Simple Authentication and Security Layer (SASL) and the Generic Security Services API (GSSAPI), plus all the tools and services that have evolved around these.

Not all operating systems use PAM. Notably, OpenBSD uses *BSD Authentication*, which spins authentication requests off into separate processes rather than dynamically linked libraries. BSD authentication separates privileges more widely than PAM, and hence reduces security risk, but is not as flexible nor as widely used.

If you want a taste of authentication administration before PAM, though, consider the variety of work needed to implement and deploy Kerberos in all your server software. While these applications all hook to a common Kerberos domain, you configure each in a completely different manner. Now imagine that, multiplied by all the authentication protocols used today, and all the interactions of those protocols with all the different software. PAM looks better now, doesn't it?

PAM Implementations

While anyone *can* implement PAM, you'll most commonly encounter three specific versions: Solaris, Linux-PAM, and OpenPAM. The different versions are almost compatible.[2]

---

2   "Almost compatible" means that anyone supporting more than one version will usually have little trouble, but occasionally subtle differences will ruin their cherub-like demeanor.

Sun first proposed PAM, and Sun Solaris had the very first implementation. The PAM code from Solaris found its way into the open source OpenSolaris, where it irrevocably became part of the public source code ecosystem. Oracle purchased Sun and no longer publicly releases any updates to the Solaris code, but community projects like OpenIndiana maintain and update a public version Solaris PAM. While other PAM implementers based their modules on Sun's original work, Sun eliminated those modules in in favor of entirely new modules. This means that the modules and configurations that appear in Linux and BSD systems, while based on Sun's work, bear no resemblance to what currently ships with Solaris PAM systems.

Linux-PAM is the Pluggable Authentication Modules implementation used for most Linux systems. It pretty closely follows the original Sun model, and many of the PAM modules keep the same names and functions of that primordial implementation. It's mostly, but not entirely, compatible with Solaris PAM. You'll find Linux-PAM primarily in Linux systems, but it also appears in some commercial Unix variants.[3] Sadly, different Linux distributions often use slightly different versions of Linux-PAM.

The author of OpenPAM attempted to include the most important parts of Linux-PAM, Solaris PAM, and the proposed XSSO standards. OpenPAM originates with the FreeBSD community. OpenPAM itself includes very few modules, but what most people call OpenPAM is really "OpenPAM and a selection of modules culled from FreeBSD." BSD-based systems that use PAM all use OpenPAM. OpenPAM's standard modules resemble those of Linux-PAM and original Solaris.

---

3   To make an SGI sysadmin scream and gibber, say "Hey, remember IRIX's two incompatible PAM stacks? Good times!"

While OS X uses OpenPAM, Apple doesn't use the common PAM modules. Instead, they've written their own PAM modules to better integrate with the One True Apple way.

Commercial UNIX systems usually have their own PAM implementation that behaves the way the vendor prefers. IBM's AIX, for example, uses the standard PAM policies but calls the pam_aix module almost everywhere. (AIX PAM is also implemented atop their proprietary Loadable Authentication Module system, because it's IBM.)

PAM Variances

Both CentOS and Debian use Linux-PAM. Sadly, they use slightly different versions of Linux-PAM. Each distribution's designers select features and modules that make sense for them. The result is, CentOS Linux-PAM includes features and options not found in Debian Linux-PAM, and vice versa. I'll mention some of those differences as we encounter them. When in doubt, consult your Linux documentation to see what toys you get.

Additionally, Linux-PAM and OpenPAM use PAM differently, because they support operating systems with different designs. For example, Linux-PAM can change the encryption algorithm used for storing new passwords. BSD and older Sun systems handle password encryption algorithms with login classes, so OpenPAM doesn't include that feature. I'll point out those differences as we go.

Linux-PAM has more knobs and buttons than OpenPAM. Part of this is because Linux-PAM needs features that OpenPAM puts elsewhere, but it also appears that the Linux-PAM developers have a fondness for extra knobs and buttons. In an effort to keep you from twiddling buttons best left alone, this book gives Linux-PAM a little more attention than OpenPAM.

While operating system vendors could coordinate their PAM configurations and come up with something that every sysadmin could immediately recognize and use, nobody's likely to do that. Instead, every open source platform welcomes other OS packagers to copy their obviously superior design. Therefore, every platform configures PAM differently.

When you first dive into an operating system's PAM setup, allocate time to understanding just how the packagers assembled everything. It's very easy to assume that the people who designed the PAM policies for an unfamiliar operating system are insane. Easy, but counterproductive. Study these unfamiliar configurations and figure out *why* they're put together that way. Not only will you understand the PAM implementation, but you'll gain insight into how the operating system packagers think—and that insight will help you master the rest of the system.

Chapter 10 illustrates how each of our three reference platforms can use one PAM module in entirely different ways, for reasons that make perfect sense to the operating system packagers.

PAM Commonalities

All these different implementations share common structure and configuration syntax. Maybe you won't initially understand *why* Debian puts a "deny all authentication" rule near the top of its default system-wide configuration, but you'll understand the syntax of the policies and be able to puzzle it out. Most PAM implementations share common module names, with a few exceptions I'll note.

One thing that every implementation and operating system installation has in common is: they have bugs. As I write this, the long-standard pam_mkhomedir module chokes and dies on CentOS. (Red Hat has reasons for this, and Chapter 6 shows how to work around it.)

The options use_first_pass and try_first_pass fail on pam_unix on FreeBSD. Always read the operating system documentation, and if something seems weird, check the mailing list archives and discussion boards for other people with the same problem. If you truly understand the numerous bugs in your preferred PAM implementation, you won't feel like laughing at the bugs in other versions.

PAM Management Tools

Some Linux distributions provide tools to manage PAM. These tools allow you to change authentication methods without editing the nasty configuration files. They work for many simple deployments. But if you want to figure out why your system behaves in a certain way, or if you want to do something complicated, these tools limit you to scenarios the tool authors imagined. And understanding weird behavior absolutely requires understanding how the rules work, both as stand-alone statements and as components of a policy.

These add-on tools overwrite the existing PAM configurations. You must either learn to compel these tools to create the needed configuration, or abandon them and manage authentication manually. In either case, understanding the configuration makes you a better sysadmin.

Target Platforms

This book mostly covers PAM as it's deployed in average Linux and BSD versions. The material on how PAM processes policies is also applicable to Oracle Solaris, OpenSolaris-derived systems, OS X, and proprietary UNIX systems, but these systems use very different core PAM modules. You can add many of the PAM modules I'll discuss to these systems, but you'll have to carefully study the configuration files.

I specifically target three operating systems with three different configuration styles: CentOS, Debian, and FreeBSD.

CentOS

CentOS is a representative of the Red Hat Linux branch of Linux. This book uses CentOS rather than official Red Hat Linux because CentOS is free and I'm a cheapskate. CentOS uses Linux-PAM. Many Linux distributions are built on top of Red Hat Linux, and those derivatives should be able to use CentOS PAM configurations.

Some PAM modules covered herein are in the EPEL package repository. To use those modules you'll need to enable that repository, build your own packages, or make other arrangements.

CentOS and related Linux distributions provide a command-line tool to configure PAM, authconfig(8).

Debian

The Debian branch of Linux has a different design philosophy than the Red Hat Linux branch. It supports much of the same software, but the management interface is almost completely different. Debian uses Linux-PAM. Many Linux distributions, such as Ubuntu and Kali Linux, are built on top of Debian, and should be able to use Debian configurations.

Some PAM modules discussed in this book are in the experimental package repository. You'll need to either enable that repo or build your own packages.

Like CentOS, Debian includes an add-on tool that writes PAM configuration files for you. Unlike CentOS, Debian uses pam-auth-update(8), a tool written by Debian folks specifically for Debian.

FreeBSD

FreeBSD is our OpenPAM reference platform. PAM-capable BSD platforms, such as Dragonfly and NetBSD, use OpenPAM, as does Apple's OS X. Configurations that work on FreeBSD should work on any BSD platform except OS X. (OS X uses completely different PAM modules than any other OpenPAM implementation, making it a special case for almost everything.)

A few Linux distributions use OpenPAM, or permit easily replacing their chosen PAM implementation with the other. You'll configure these operating systems much like any other PAM implementation, but you might find some PAM modules have slightly different names. If you're using a Linux distribution with OpenPAM and get confused looking for a module, check the CentOS or Debian examples to find the name the Linux folks assign to that module.

Other Platforms

PAM might not be a monolithic standard, but the basics of its configuration are common across implementations. Sysadmins managing Solaris derivatives or OS X can use the guidance in here to create their own PAM configurations.

Much of the guidance on add-on PAM modules, such as Google Authenticator or SSH agent authentication, applies directly to every platform. The details of configuring a password quality checker don't vary much between operating systems, even if where you place that module in a policy differs.

PAM and OpenSSH

OpenSSH's SSH server sshd(8) doesn't really need PAM. The industry standard method for SSH authentication—keys—doesn't fit within PAM. The SSH server does need to check passwords, which does involve PAM somewhere along the way, but it's a simple-minded check. If you're using one-factor authentication, the simple password check works just fine.

If you want more complicated PAM-based authentication, though, start by telling sshd(8) to link with PAM. Set the `UsePAM` option in *sshd_config* to *yes*. This enables PAM-based account access checks, automatic home directory completion, and so on. It will not trigger PAM-based authentication, however.

The SSH daemon has two options for handling user authentication at the keyboard. One, `PasswordAuthentication`, is specifically for passwords. The other, `ChallengeResponseAuthentication`, is a more generic authentication mechanism. To use PAM, you almost certainly want `ChallengeResponseAuthentication`.

```
UsePAM yes
ChallengeResponseAuthentication yes
PasswordAuthentication no
```

Console and serial port login attempts use the login(8) program, which has its own PAM policy. The SSH server can pass part of the user login process to login(8) with the `UseLogin` option. This option is normally *no*. Interactions between login(8) and sshd(8) policies are either highly amusing or utterly infuriating, depending on if you're the one who needs to make them work. To use PAM, it's best to let the SSH server handle the login process rather than calling up login(8).

```
UseLogin no
```

Finally, tell sshd(8) to consult with PAM on authentication. For that, you need the `AuthenticationMethods` option in *sshd_config*. The `keyboard-interactive` setting tells `sshd` to pass authentication through to another agent, such as PAM. If you activate PAM and you tell sshd(8) to use `keyboard-interactive` authentication, you'll get PAM for authentication as well as account management.

Setting it to `publickey` means `sshd` requires public key authentication. Combining the two with a comma means that `sshd` requires both, while separating them with a space means `sshd` offers a choice of authentication options.

Most people who want to enable PAM in sshd(8) want the daemon to reject all authentication requests without a public key, and then give PAM a chance to either permit or veto the connection. That gives you an AuthenticationMethods entry like this.

```
AuthenticationMethods publickey,keyboard-interactive
```

Alternatively, you might want to let users with public key authentication right in, and then fall back to PAM for one-time passwords or some other strong authentication. Put a space between the methods.

```
AuthenticationMethods publickey keyboard-interactive
```

Even with these options, not all PAM modules work with `sshd`. Plugging pam_ssh_agent_auth (Chapter 8) into `sshd`, as amusing as that might sound, will only annoy you.

PAM, LDAP, and Kerberos

Any time sysadmins ponder authentication, the topic of centralized authentication comes up. Most of these discussions wind up with various permutations of Lightweight Directory Access Protocol (LDAP) and Kerberos. Will this book help you with these?

Yes… and no.

The difficulty of deploying LDAP has very little to do with PAM. Configuring LDAP authentication is hard because LDAP is so wildly free-form. You can use any number of LDAP schemas or create your own. Decisions made early in your LDAP deployment have repercussions that you'll live with forever. Worse, differences between the LDAP modules on each of our reference platforms mean that each platform needs a unique configuration.

Kerberos is less free-form than LDAP, but it has very specific requirements and higher overhead.

This book will help you understand how your PAM configuration affects these centralized authentication methods. It will help you extract debugging information from PAM as you deploy. It won't help you decide how to design your LDAP schema.

Book Overview

This book has two big pieces. The first six chapters guide you through how PAM works.

Chapter 0 is this introduction.

Chapter 1, "PAM Components," discusses the parts of PAM. You'll learn about PAM configuration files and statements, the control statements, PAM modules, and common flags. We'll also explore how PAM policies work, and how PAM decides to allow or reject requests.

Chapter 2, "Common Modules," covers modules everyone needs to understand, such as those used for traditional Unix authentication, permitting root to access services, accounting, and more.

Chapter 3, "PAM Items, Codes, and Functions," dives into some PAM internals. A sysadmin doesn't need to program PAM, but does need to recognize these codes when they show up. Understanding PAM items and return codes is critical to managing PAM.

Chapter 4, "Linux-PAM Extended Controls and Substacks," discusses Linux-PAM extensions to PAM configuration, such as substacks and making decisions based on specific PAM responses.

Chapter 5, "Popular Linux-PAM Modules," goes into detail on modules usually deployed in Linux-PAM systems. Linux configures features in PAM that other systems place elsewhere.

Chapter 6, "PAM Debugging," shows how to find problems in your PAM configuration.

With these six chapters, you can perform essential configuration tasks and debugging. The remainder of the book takes you into specific modules. A trivial Internet search uncovers hundreds of PAM modules, but this book covers only a few. Some of them are very widely available and very useful, such as pam_exec (Chapter 7). Some are popular, such as pam_ssh_agent_auth (Chapter 8) and Google Authenticator (Chapter 9). Some let me illustrate important points about PAM. The module pam_ssh (Chapter 10) not only illustrates a useful feature, but also serves as a case study on the infuriating differences in how operating systems deploy identical PAM modules.

This still leaves hundreds of PAM modules. Many PAM modules are vital to the people who need them, but only a fraction of readers need any given module. This book gives you enough understanding of PAM to feel assured of your ability to write correct rules for using that module, freeing your precious brainpower to understand the module itself and how that module fits into a policy.

Chapter 7, "Arbitrary Files and Random Programs," discusses permitting access based on a text list. You also learn about running external programs as part of PAM.

Chapter 8, "SSH Agent Authentication," covers using your SSH agent to authenticate to services after logging onto the system.

Chapter 9, "One-Time Passwords: Google Authenticator," helps you implement time-based, one-time passwords (TOTP) using Google's PAM module and a variety of client software.

Chapter 10, "Console Access with SSH Keys," teaches you how to configure a workstation so users can use their SSH keys as part of the local authentication process.

Chapter 11, "Password Quality Checks," discusses using PAM modules to limit passwords users can choose.

Grab your flashlight. We're going into PAM.

Chapter 1: PAM Components

Any PAM system handles the login and authentication process with several types of rules. We'll start with the configuration files that contain the rules, then dive into the authentication components and the actions.

PAM Configuration Files

You might find PAM configurations in the file `/etc/pam.conf`, or in a whole mess of files in the `/etc/pam.d/` directory.

When Solaris spawned PAM back in the 1990s, a single configuration file sufficed for the few services that used PAM. Each PAM rule statement started with the name of the service that rule applied to. The rules for access to rlogind(8) started with `rsh`, the rules managing telnet access started with `telnet`, and so on. Solaris-derived systems still use a single `pam.conf`.

PAM spread like bindweed, though. Before long, the single configuration file constrained and complicated systems administration. Implementations like Linux-PAM and OpenPAM split PAM rules out into the `/etc/pam.d` directory, where each service had a file named after it. Instead of starting a rule with the word `rlogin`, Linux-PAM and OpenPAM put the rules for rlogind(8) in `/etc/pam.d/rsh`, the rules for SSH access in `/etc/pam.d/sshd`, and so on.

FreeBSD systems also separate configuring core system components and add-on packages. While the PAM configurations for system components live in /etc/pam.d, add-on packages have their PAM configurations in /usr/local/etc/pam.d. You might find similar variations in other operating systems.

Systems that use /etc/pam.d are far more common than those relying on /etc/pam.conf. The examples in this book assume you're using per-service PAM configuration files. If you're on a Solaris-based system, you'll need to add the service name to the front of every PAM rule in /etc/pam.conf.

PAM Policies

If you've never looked at a PAM file, go look at one of the files in /etc/pam.d/. A policy file has a bunch of statements like this.

```
auth        required  pam_unix.so        no_warn try_first_pass nullok
account     required  pam_unix.so
session     required  pam_lastlog.so  no_fail
password    required  pam_unix.so        no_warn try_first_pass
```

Each line is one PAM statement or rule. Each statement contains four components: the type, the control, the module, and the module arguments. The first PAM statement shown here has the type *auth*, the control *required*, the module *pam_unix.so*, and the arguments *no_warn*, *try_first_pass*, and *nullok*.

We'll go over each of these in detail, but understanding the basics of each will help you understand how the parts interoperate as we dive deeper.

A *type* is a component of the authentication process. Managing credentials is a part of authentication. So is setting up a user's account and resource limits, as well as changing the user's password.

The *control* statement indicates how PAM should react to success and failure of a PAM module. Should the authentication request be granted? Should the request try the next module? Should a failure here terminate the whole process? These control statements provide PAM's logic.

The *module* is the PAM module being used. Use the filename of the module, including the trailing `.so`. (OpenPAM allows you to omit the `.so`.) Most PAM modules get installed in a system-specific location, such as `/usr/lib/` or `/lib/x86_64-linux-gnu/security/`. If you want to use a module that's not in a standard directory, list it by its full path. Listing a module here tells PAM to feed the authentication information to this module and collect a response. For example, pam_unix.so checks the local system's password file for a valid username and password. If PAM hands this module a username and password, the module will respond either "yes, it exists" or "nope, invalid." The control statement tells PAM what to do for each kind of response. (A module can respond with more than "yes" or "no," as discussed in Chapter 4.)

The *module arguments* are specific to each module. Some arguments, like no_warn and debug, are recognized by many modules. The exact meaning of each depends on the module, however. Not all modules need or use arguments. A few poorly coded modules object to having any arguments at all.

Split long statements between lines with a backslash (\).

```
auth   required  pam_echo checking OPIE RUSER=%U \
   USER=%u TTY=%t SERVICE=%s RHOST=%H
```

Let's dive into authentication types.

Authentication Types

PAM divides the authentication process into four components. These components might be called *facilities* or *types*, depending on whose documentation you read. The type is the first field in a PAM rule.

The *auth*, or authentication, type verifies the authentication information presented and establishes any restrictions or resource limits set for the account. If you enter a wrong password or a non-existent username, the auth type kicks you out. If a user account has a limited number of processes, can use a maximum amount of memory, or belongs to particular groups, the auth type handles setting those limits.

The *account* type controls access to an account as dictated by characteristics other than simple authentication. If the user can log in only on February 28th of odd-numbered years, that's configured in the account type. A user might enter the proper authentication information, but if no account's available she cannot log in.

The *session* type handles system-side setup needed to provide service. A command-line user needs a virtual terminal, a home directory, and probably a log entry saying that they logged in. An anonymous FTP user doesn't need a virtual terminal, personal home directory, or a shell, but does need FTP-specific resources. When the session ends, any allocated resources need to be torn down. The session type manages all such per-session requirements.

Finally, the *password* type is needed when the user's credentials need updating on the system. Maybe the user is changing their password. Maybe their hardware token needs poking. The password type handles any actions needed to update the authentication credentials.

Each service a host offers might have one or more statement of each type. Depending on how authentication should work on your system, you might have dozens of one type, a single statement of two other types, and none of the fourth.

A group of statements of the same type is often called a *chain* or sometimes a *stack*. This book uses the word *policy*. Look at the example PAM policy at the beginning of this chapter. Each policy is only one statement long. In the next section, we'll see policies with several statements.

With Linux-PAM, you'll occasionally see type statements with a leading hyphen before the name: *-auth, -account, -session*, and *-password*. These indicate that if the module is not installed on the system, PAM should ignore the error. You'll see this when a module is optional, such as for Kerberos or systemd(8).

PAM Controls

PAM controls declare how a particular module affects a policy. You can decide which types of authentication are mandatory, which are voluntary, and which you don't care about.

PAM sends the user's authentication information to each module in the policy. Each module returns either success or failure, meaning that the authentication attempt succeeds or fails for that module. For example, a password-verification module determines if the password provided by the user matches the password configured for that user. If the password matches, the module returns a success; if not, a failure. The PAM module responsible for user home directories looks to see if the user's home directory exists, and returns success if it's there and failure if it's not. (PAM modules can return more than these two codes, as discussed in Chapter 4, but this gets you started.)

PAM controls don't resemble the strict allow/deny syntax you'll find in applications like packet filters, web servers, and other Access Control Lists. They're more like a long-standing committee in a centuries-old educational institution steeped in tradition and ritual, where each member has an unusual name, baroque responsibilities, and unique privileges.

This committee votes on authentication in a specified, stately order. Each member has specific ways they can vote. Perhaps the Archchancellor starts the vote, and can either say "yes" or reject the whole proposal before anyone else gets a chance. The Dean can vote "no comment" or "no," but doesn't have the right to vote in favor of anything. The Senior Wrangler can vote either "no" or "yes, so long as nobody else objects." If voting reaches as far as the Lecturer in Recent Runes, he can either stay silent or declare, "yes, dang it, and the vote's over, I win!"

Meanwhile, the Librarian has a seat at the table but can only take notes and eat peanuts.

Control statements formally define this structure. Each PAM module gets certain voting privileges. Some control statements say, "if this module returns success, stop processing and immediately allow authentication." Other control statements give instructions like "if this fails, terminate immediately" or "if this module succeeds, proceed to the next module." At the end of the policy, the vote determines if access is granted or denied.

Linux-PAM users can access a more complex control syntax, as discussed in Chapter 4. Even so, most Linux-PAM deployments still rely heavily on these "traditional" control statements.

PAM has five main controls: *required*, *requisite*, *optional*, *sufficient*, and *binding*.

Required

A statement with the *required* control means that this module must return success for the policy to permit access. If a user enters the wrong password, they cannot log in. If the sysadmin has configured the host so that nobody can log in, they cannot log in.

If a required control fails, PAM processes the remaining modules in the policy. The login stills return a failure, denying access, but other modules get a chance to do any logging or accounting that they require.

If a required module succeeds, PAM continues processing the policy, giving some other module a chance to deny access.

Every required module must succeed for PAM to allow access. If even one required module fails, success in the other modules doesn't suffice. Consider this sample policy.

```
auth   required   pam_breathalyzer.so
auth   required   pam_ddr.so
auth   required   pam_genescan.so
```

This policy first hands the authentication information to the pam_breathalyzer.so module[4], then to pam_ddr.so, and then to pam_genescan.so, all with the required control. This policy requires unanimous consent. If any one of these modules returns a failure, the authentication request fails. All three modules get processed, though, so they can perform secondary tasks like logging information helpful for the sysadmin.

Depending on the module's function and the policy type, required statements are a key part of multi-factor authentication.

Many other control statements (described later) claim to grant access if they succeed. If an earlier required module fails, though, PAM rejects the access. A failed required control acts as the great big hammer of "nope."

Requisite

The *requisite* control indicates that the module must succeed for access to be granted.

If a requisite control succeeds, PAM continues processing modules. The request is granted unless later rejected.

If a requisite control fails, PAM immediately stops processing modules and tells the application that the request is rejected. This makes requisite different from required.

---

4   Yes, the breathalyzer module should probably test to see if the user is sober enough to log in, and thus be in an account policy. It's just an example, go with it.

Let's examine this PAM policy with the requisite control.

```
auth   required  pam_breathalyzer.so
auth   requisite pam_ddr.so
auth   required  pam_genescan.so
```

The first module, pam_breathalyzer.so, is required. If the user does not pass the breathalyzer test, she cannot log in, period. Whether that module succeeds or fails, PAM continues to the next module in the policy.

The second module, pam_ddr.so, is requisite. It must succeed for PAM to grant access. If this module fails, PAM immediately stops processing the policy and tells the application that authentication is refused.

The third module, pam_genescan.so, is also required. The third module is only triggered if the second module succeeds, however. A failure in pam_ddr.so means pam_genescan.so doesn't get checked.

Using the requisite control can give the user hints as to where the authentication attempt failed. An intruder can use this information to more precisely target their attacks. Use requisite only when you have a very specific reason to not run later controls. Do not expend time, energy, or attention optimizing login failures. This policy uses the requisite control because gene scanning is expensive, and avoiding it unnecessarily saves money.

Optional

Statements with the *optional* control have little effect on success or failure. Operating systems use `optional` controls to manage functions that might or might not be deployed or configured, such as SSH agents and Kerberos. You'll also deploy optional controls to add additional functions to an authentication session.

An optional control can permit or deny access if and only if no other module in the policy expresses an opinion. If you have a bunch of sufficient statements and an optional statement, and none of the sufficient statements permit access, the optional statement can permit or deny access.

Here's a policy that uses an optional control.

```
auth   required   pam_breathalyzer.so
auth   required   pam_ddr.so
auth   required   pam_genescan.so
auth   optional   pam_faildelay.so
```

Our three sample modules are still required: all must succeed for the user to get access.

The new module, pam_faildelay.so, sets a delay between login attempts. If a user's attempt to log in gets rejected, the module delays returning an authentication prompt to the user by several seconds. This module doesn't do anything with the user's authentication credentials. As it only changes how PAM behaves, you'd expect it to always return success. In the unlikely event that pam_faildelay.so fails, however, you don't want the failure to prevent logins.

Statements with an optional control normally go at the front of a policy. You probably wouldn't want the failure of a requisite control to block the optional module. I deliberately put pam_faildelay at the end of this policy, however. I don't want to introduce a delay before the first logon attempt.

I should mention that using pam_faildelay at all is a poor idea; such delays should be built into the application, not provided through PAM, as assorted security advisories show. Ideally, each authentication attempt should take a constant amount of time, rather than providing a constant delay between attempts. It's a popular module, though, so you'll need to at least recognize it.

The session type is the most common user of optional controls.

Sufficient

The *sufficient* control means that success in this module is enough to provide access, provided a previous `required` control hasn't failed.

If a sufficient control succeeds, PAM immediately grants access. It does not process further modules in the policy.

If a sufficient control fails, PAM does not deny access. Failure of a sufficient control gets treated like failure of an optional control. PAM records this failure as an optional failure. Not triggering a failure permits the user to try another authentication method. Consider the following policy.

```
auth   sufficient   pam_breathalyzer.so
auth   sufficient   pam_ddr.so
auth   sufficient   pam_genescan.so
```

All three modules are sufficient, meaning that successfully authenticating to any one of them immediately permits access.

Think about this policy for a moment. We have three chances to create success, but the only failures this policy can create are optional. What does your PAM implementation do when there's no explicit acceptance or denial? OpenPAM defaults to rejecting the request. Linux-PAM normally rejects the request, but in the last twenty years I've encountered certain configurations and distributions that permit access unless specifically denied. Best practice calls for explicitly rejecting access. Both Linux-PAM and OpenPAM include pam_deny for exactly this application.

All requests to pam_deny fail, creating a fail-safe. If your last rule in a policy uses a sufficient control, follow it up with a required pam_deny statement. You'll get more detail on pam_deny in Chapter 3.

```
auth   sufficient   pam_breathalyzer.so
auth   sufficient   pam_ddr.so
auth   sufficient   pam_genescan.so
auth   required     pam_deny.so
```

With this addition, either one of these tests passes or the request is denied.

The sufficient control permits either/or authentication methods. Look at our next policy for an example.

```
auth   sufficient   pam_breathalyzer.so
auth   required     pam_ddr.so
auth   required     pam_genescan.so
```

The first module, pam_breathalyzer.so, is sufficient. If the user passes this module, PAM considers the request successful and stops processing the policy. If this module fails, though, PAM logs an optional failure and continues down the policy.

The second and third statements are required. You'll hit these statements only if the first module returns a failure.

The end result? The user may authenticate either with pam_breathalyzer.so, or with both pam_ddr.so and pam_genescan. so. As this policy ends with required controls, we don't need a failsafe pam_deny.so statement at the end.

Binding

The *binding* control is pretty much a `required` control that immediately stops processing the policy on success. The binding control is used rarely at best—I have never seen it deployed in the real world. The Sun engineers thought binding looked useful when they first proposed the standard, but reality disagreed. I've only seen the word "bind" in PAM statements in an LDAP context. It's not even implemented in Linux-PAM. For these reasons, while I'll explain binding here, the rest of this book pretends it doesn't exist.

If a statement with a binding control succeeds, and no earlier required statement failed, the application is told to immediately grant access. PAM does not process any further statements in the policy.

If a statement with a binding control fails, PAM denies access. The remaining rules of the policy are processed, allowing them to perform their functions, but the access request is ultimately rejected.

If you're considering using binding, try sufficient instead.

Include

Both Linux-PAM and OpenPAM support *include* statements, allowing you to pull one policy into another. The policy could come from files in `/etc/pam.d` or `/etc/pam.conf`. Debian systems pull in the entire file that's referenced, while OpenPAM and most Linux-PAM systems pull in only the statements of the relevant type. Here's CentOS' `/etc/pam.d/sudo`, the PAM configuration for sudo(1).

```
auth       include     system-auth
account    include     system-auth
password   include     system-auth
session    optional    pam_keyinit.so revoke
session    required    pam_limits.so
```

This policy has a single auth rule. It includes the policy `system-auth`. This tells PAM to check for a file `/etc/pam.d/system-auth` or a policy of that name in `/etc/pam.conf`, grab all of the rules of this type, and put them here. The file `/etc/pam.d/system-auth` contains this auth policy.

```
auth   required    pam_env.so
auth   sufficient  pam_fprintd.so
auth   sufficient  pam_unix.so nullok try_first_pass
auth   requisite   pam_succeed_if.so uid >= 1000 quiet_success
auth   required    pam_deny.so
```

When a user accesses the login service, they pass through this policy.

Using includes lets the sysadmin maintain the PAM configuration for several services in one location. Changing the included file makes changes immediately propagate to all involved services.

All operating systems use a slightly different include policy design, however. Many CentOS PAM modules include the `system-auth` configuration file. FreeBSD uses `/etc/pam.d/system`. Debian breaks the central include files out by types, such as `common-auth`, `common-session`, and so on.

Debian uses @include to pull in an entire file. Here's Debian's `/etc/pam.d/sudo` configuration.

```
@include common-auth
@include common-account
@include common-session-noninteractive
```

This configuration says "use the same authentication as everyone else, the same account type as everything else, and the same session setup as any other noninteractive process."

The advantage to including files like this is it makes adding entries to the beginning or end of a policy very easy. If I want to add a PAM module to a type for only one program, I can add it to that program's file. Here, I tell Debian's `sudo` to require a breathalyzer test in addition to all the usual authentication methods.

```
auth   required   pam_breathalyzer.so
@include common-auth
@include common-account
@include common-session-noninteractive
```

Include files improve your flexibility without requiring that you maintain multiple copies of your PAM policies.

Linux-PAM also supports *substacks*, which are similar to includes. See Chapter 4 for a discussion of substacks.

Modules and Arguments

The modules and their arguments at the end of each PAM statement dictate the functionality or behavior the rule implements. Each module provides features such as checking passwords, configuring home directories, or allocating terminals.

We'll install most features by installing and using PAM modules.

Module Context

As you explore PAM modules, you'll notice that many modules get called by several different PAM types. The pam_unix.so module, for example, appears in auth, account, and password policies. The way the module behaves, and the services it provides, vary depending on the type calling it. If an auth type calls pam_unix.so, the module checks the password. The account type gets account availability information from pam_unix.so. The password type uses pam_unix.so to change the system password file.

Not every module provides services to all types. Some very useful modules support only one type but perform a vital service for that type. The module pam_mkhomedir.so, for example, creates nonexistent home directories for authenticated users as part of the session type. This has nothing to do with passwords, but is vital for large enterprises.

Module Arguments

Module *arguments*, or *flags*, configure the module itself. Should a module tell a user why it rejected a request, or not? Do you want optional features activated? Module arguments enable and disable these optional features.

Here, we set the nullok and try_first_pass flags to the pam_unix module.

```
auth  sufficient  pam_unix.so  nullok try_first_pass
```

Some flags take their own arguments, letting you set limits or toggle functions.

```
account  required  pam_breathalyzer.so  bal<8
account  required  pam_genescan.so  neanderthal=0
```

Breathalyzers on their own don't know your organization's tolerance for alcohol. In this example, if a user's blood alcohol level is less than 0.08, the account is available. How did I learn about this argument? I read the module documentation. Similarly, in compliance with United States anti-discrimination laws, we're telling the gene scanner to not perform the Neanderthal checks.

A module might need a completely different argument when used in a different context.

Common Module Arguments

While anyone can write a PAM module, that doesn't mean that everyone reinvents module configuration. Most PAM modules accept these usual arguments for common functionality.

A PAM module isn't required to accept any of these arguments. A properly coded PAM module that doesn't support the functionality of a flag will silently ignore it.

debug

The *debug* flag tells the module to log debugging information via syslog. PAM debugging messages are logged with the auth facility at priority debug. Adding the debug flag to pam_unix.so and watching the system log will teach you a whole bunch about how your PAM implementation processes authentication requests.

Most but not all PAM modules support debugging. If a PAM module behaves badly when you use the debug flag, take that as a hint that the module is poorly programmed. You might be stuck using the module, but at least you've been warned.

In OpenPAM, the debug flag not only triggers debugging output of PAM behavior, but debugging within the shared library. You'll see which service function gets called and what it returns, as discussed in Chapter 3.

Generic PAM errors, like listing a module that doesn't exist, appear in the system's security log (normally `/var/log/secure` or `/var/log/auth`).

no_warn

PAM modules might offer feedback on why they reject an access request. Enabling *no_warn* silences that feedback. While the breathalyzer module normally tells a user that they can't log in because they're too intoxicated to find their face, let alone program, adding no_warn turns that warning off.

use_first_pass

A host's authentication system might be set up to try to validate a username and password through each of several methods. One host might try both the local password file and LDAP, for example. While each PAM module could prompt the user for the password, the *use_first_pass* option tells the module to use an already entered password. Without this option, it's possible that a module will prompt the user for their password again.

If the user has never entered a password, she gets prompted anyway.

If the existing password doesn't work, the module fails.

The use_first_pass option normally appears only in auth rules.

try_first_pass

Much like use_first_pass, the *try_first_pass* option tells the module to try to authenticate with a previously entered password. If the password isn't correct, however, the module can prompt the user for a password. If that password fails, the module fails.

The try_first_pass option normally appears only in auth rules.

use_mapped_pass

The *use_mapped_pass* option lets you hash or encrypt a password entered by the user. Like the binding control, use_mapped_pass is rarely used today. I'm only including it for completeness.

expose_account

Human beings are terrible at following instructions. The machine asks for a username, and we type a password. For reasons like this, modules tend to be quiet about failures. They keep quiet about information such as the username, the user's home directory, and so on. The *expose_account* option tells the module to release this information. Some modules will print messages like `failed to authenticate user mwl` or `home directory /home/mwl not available` when you enable this option.

Support for expose_account varies between modules.

Default Policies

Not all applications need their own policy. Many applications can share a set of common defaults. If PAM doesn't find a policy file for an application, it calls the "other" policy, from `/etc/pam.d/other`.

These system default policies vary widely between systems. FreeBSD's is very similar to the `system` policy file that gets pulled into most other policies, while CentOS' denies everything. Check what your operating system does.

Policy Processing and Results

A *PAM policy*, or *chain*, is a group of rules of the same type for a service. An application might have auth, account, session, and password policies, or it might have policies for only some of those. FTP doesn't need (and shouldn't grow!) a way for users to change passwords, after all.

Here's the complete default system authentication from a FreeBSD system.

```
auth       sufficient  pam_opie.so            no_warn no_fake_prompts
auth       requisite   pam_opieaccess.so      no_warn allow_local
auth       required    pam_unix.so            no_warn try_first_pass nullok
account    required    pam_login_access.so
account    required    pam_unix.so
session    required    pam_lastlog.so         no_fail
password   required    pam_unix.so            no_warn try_first_pass
```

The auth policy is three statements long. The account policy is two statements, while session and password are only a single statement. Policies can be far, far longer—on most Linux systems auth policies are at least half a dozen statements, with more added on a per-protocol basis. Apple and OpenSolaris-based systems often have one-statement policies. (That's why we're going through a modest OpenPAM example here.)

Each policy has the task of allowing or rejecting that type of access request. It makes the decision based on the statements in the policy.

Consider the three-statement auth policy above. When a user runs a program that invokes this policy, PAM first calls the module pam_opie and feeds it the required information. The pam_opie module has the sufficient control: if it's successful, the auth policy immediately says "Access allowed" and stops processing the policy. A failure from this first module doesn't mean that the module objects to letting the user log in—it simply won't say yes. When a sufficient module fails, PAM continues processing the policy. It's the computing equivalent of "go ask your mother."

The second auth module, pam_opieaccess, has the requisite control. If this module returns success, access is allowed. If the module returns failure, though, PAM immediately stops processing the policy and returns failure. It's a hard yes/no decision.

The last module in the auth policy, pam_unix, is required. If the module returns success, access is allowed. If the module returns failure, access is denied.

Taken as a whole, the auth policy could be processed in a couple ways. If the first, sufficient module succeeds, access is immediately allowed. If it fails, processing falls through to the next two rules in the policy. Both of these must return success for access to be permitted. A failure in either of the last two modules denies access.

In most deployments, policies weigh rejection more heavily than permitting access. Most control types have veto power, letting them deny access even if later statements in the policy say yes.

As you can see, PAM policy processing differs from the usual allow/deny syntax of your average access control list. Thinking of PAM policies as resembling firewall rules will cause you pain. PAM uses its special language to make that clear.

Now that you understand some basics of how PAM works, let's look at a few common modules and see how they're configured.

Chapter 2: Common Modules

While Linux-PAM and OpenPAM were separately implemented, their developers used Solaris PAM as a model. Both include many modules similar in concept to those in older versions of Solaris.

This chapter takes you through many of those common modules, how they work, and what you can do with them. Many of these are very small and provide only a single function, but I cover them briefly so that you start to understand how PAM glues together all the disparate Unix authentication functions.

Let's start with a class you'll see everywhere.

Core Unix Authentication: pam_unix

The *pam_unix* module handles all interactions with the system password file, `/etc/passwd`, and related files like `/etc/group`, `/etc/master.passwd`, `/etc/shadow`, and so on. It also supports Network Information Service (NIS), the traditional means of managing distributed authentication. A host not using a centralized authentication system like LDAP or Kerberos almost certainly uses pam_unix. Even hosts that use centralized authentication often use pam_unix to look up unprivileged accounts for local applications.

The auth, account, and password PAM types use pam_unix. It's not used for the session type.

Password authentication predates PAM by decades. The pam_unix module has the unenviable duty of lugging around all those years of accumulated functionality, controlled by various option flags.

Detailed Logging with audit

The *audit* option is a more detailed and verbose version of the debug option. It sends very detailed logging to syslog, using facility auth and priority debug.

Depending on the operating system, the version of PAM, and the server program, the audit log might not contain much useful information. The OpenSSH server, for example, doesn't necessarily use PAM at all.

Empty Passwords

The general rule with authentication is: no password, no access. Accounts without passwords are not generally meant to be used interactively. Application accounts, like those for MySQL or nginx and so on, often don't have passwords. (Application accounts are also locked, prohibiting logons.) New user accounts might not have a password on them.

In some cases, you might want to allow someone to log on as one of these users. The *nullok* option permits access to such accounts without a password.

Some implementations, notably CentOS, use nullok in an auth rule to permit users to log on without a password. They then add nullok to a password rule, as shown below. The combination lets the new user log on, but forces them to immediately change their password. If you're interested in this feature, see if your PAM install supports this behavior.

```
auth       sufficient   pam_unix.so nullok try_first_pass
password   sufficient   pam_unix.so sha512 shadow \
                        nullok try_first_pass use_authtok
```

The downside of this behavior is that anyone can log onto the new user's account and assign a password. You have no guarantee that the new account actually goes to the intended person. But the alternatives are all bad: Assign all the new users the same password, like "sword-fish?"[5] Generate random strings and hope the hapless person can type them correctly?

Debian's Linux-PAM supports the *nullok_secure* option, which permits access with an empty password if it's used on a secure termi-nal. A secure terminal is one you've determined to be in a physically safe space, such as a locked data center. It's a convenience for locations you've identified as secure. Secure terminals are generally limited to the console, virtual terminals, and various types of serial ports, and are listed in `/etc/securetty`.

Password File Configuration

Most Linux systems expect PAM to configure the local password data-base. They use the system-wide PAM configuration to tell the system to use a shadow password file, which hashing algorithm to use for passwords, and so on.

I strongly encourage everyone to leave these settings at their de-faults. You want your hosts to use a shadow password file. Your knowl-edge of cryptographic hashing algorithms compares poorly to that of the people who made those selections for your operating system. You might have heard that Blowfish is cool[6], but Linux distributions use SHA 512 for a really good reason. If you think you must change the password configuration, you're wrong.

---

5   The password is always "swordfish."
6   Blowfish grow spines when you try to eat them. If you eat them anyway, without knowing how to cut the poison sac out, you fall over dead. Blowfish are mean little critters. Doesn't mean I'd use a blowfish as armor.

Users who change passwords often try to get away with minor changes, such as scrambling the letters or adding a digit. Debian uses the *obscure* option to check for these basic problems when changing a password. This option isn't supported in CentOS or OpenPAM, but quality-checking modules provide better service.

Group Membership

A really common goal is limiting authentication by group. The most well-known example is how many systems permit only members of the group **wheel** to use su(1) to become **root**. Linux-PAM's *pam_wheel* and the *pam_group* included in OpenPAM systems let you check for group membership[7]. Despite the different names, you configure them in an almost identical manner.

First, which group are you going to check? As you might guess from the name, pam_wheel checks for membership in the **wheel** group, while pam_group has no default. For either module, specify the desired group with the *group* option.

```
auth requisite pam_group.so group=wheel
```

It makes sense to allow only certain users to access the **root** account, but you might want users to be able to access other accounts. On an Oracle database server, for example, the database team probably needs to switch to the **oracle** user on a regular basis. Eliminating su(1) access for the DBAs would cause you a whole bunch of grief. The *root_only* option tells both modules to apply this statement only if the user is trying to become **root**.

You can also use group checks to block access based on group. The *deny* option reverses the meaning of the group check, so that if a user

---

7   Linux-PAM also has a pam_group, but it has a completely different function than OpenPAM's pam_group. Because programmers hate us lowly sysadmins.

is a member of a group he cannot access the service. You might, say, block the **customer** group from accessing SSH with an entry like this in */etc/pam.d/sshd*.

```
auth required pam_wheel.so group=customers deny
```

Negative checks like this are riskier than positive checks. I recommend only permitting access to a group member, rather than denying people in a group. Forget to add the new employee to the **staff** group and she can't do her job—but you'll notice right away. Forget to add the new client to the customer group, and she silently gets access to a forbidden service.

Linux-PAM also supports the *trust* option. If a user is part of the specified group, she doesn't have to enter a password. With trust, a member of the **wheel** group can run su root without entering a password.

Group checks normally use the original user's group membership to perform checks. You can invert this check, creating an "allow this service if the *target* is a member of this group," with the *luser* option[8]. You could thus create PAM configurations like "allow su(1) to the **oracle** account."

OpenPAM's pam_group also has a *fail_safe* option. Setting fail_safe tells pam_group that if the specified group doesn't exist or has no members, it should permit access. You might use this when centrally managing your PAM configuration. You can't use fail_safe with the **wheel** group, though.

Other pam_unix Options

The standard debug option is useful, as are use_first_pass and try_first_pass. OpenPAM's pam_unix does not support try_first_pass, however.

_____

8   I've been assured that *luser* means "local user," not anything else that might come to mind.

Allowing and Denying Requests

When building PAM policies, ending a policy with a firm *yes* or *no* can help. PAM includes two modules for exactly that.

pam_deny

Sometimes, you just gotta say no. That's what *pam_deny* is for.

Use pam_deny to block all requests. By putting pam_deny at the end of a policy, you declare that everything not permitted earlier is forbidden.

The pam_deny module is especially important when using sufficient statements. The sufficient control says "pass this and you're in, so long as nobody else objects. Fail this, and you can try something else." If a request reaches the end of a bunch of sufficient statements and hasn't passed any of them, but nothing has denied access, adding a pam_deny at the end provides an authoritative refusal.

You'll also see pam_deny used where a request simply makes no sense. CentOS provides fingerprint-based authentication. The Red Hat developers believe that people's fingerprints don't change,[9] so they categorically deny attempts to change the user's password.

```
password     required      pam_deny.so
```

The required control indicates that the module must return success for the request to be granted. The pam_deny module never returns success. This PAM configuration blocks all attempts to change the user's fingerprint.

pam_permit

If pam_deny is uptight and refuses everything, *pam_permit* is its mirror twin. Like a really bad negotiator, pam_permit says yes to everything. It has no options and no tunable behavior.

---

9   The Red Hat developers clearly need to read more crime novels or watch more John Carpenter movies.

Some services need to use pam_permit to explicitly allow access. You'll see many programs use pam_permit with session policies for this reason.

Allowing Root

PAM lets you explicitly grant the **root** account its all-encompassing privilege. The *pam_rootok* module allows access if the user is **root**.

I most often see pam_rootok used with include statements. Here's the CentOS 7 PAM configuration for chfn(1).

```
auth      sufficient  pam_rootok.so
auth      include     system-auth
account   include     system-auth
password  include     system-auth
session   include     system-auth
```

Taken as a whole, this means "**root** can always run this command, or others as the system authentication permits."

Pam_rootok works only for auth statements.

Secure Terminals

Unix-like systems consider some terminals more secure than others. While SSH might be a secure protocol, the virtual terminal used by SSH is not inherently secure. The physical console might not be in a secure location, but if you have console access you can physically alter the machine, so you might as well call it secure. Those serial ports might be secure if they're connected to a local terminal on the sysadmin's desk, but not so much if they're in a modem pool. If the machine and its console are in a room secured by very serious locks, the physical terminal is as secure as it can be.

Normally, a user cannot log in directly as **root**. They need to log in as a regular user, and then use su(1) to become **root**. The *pam_securetty* module allows a direct login as **root**, if and only if the user authenticates on a secure terminal.

BSD systems consider a terminal device secure if its entry in `/etc/ttys` has the *secure* flag.

Linux systems list secure terminal devices in `/etc/securettys`. Linux-PAM's pam_securetty also allows logins as **root** on console devices listed on the kernel command line, as well as consoles listed in `/sys/class/tty/console/active`. Pam_securetty's *noconsole* option disallows these additional devices, restricting **root** logins to only devices listed in `/etc/securettys`.

Login Accounting

PAM provides information to the user accounting system through the *pam_lastlog* module. On CentOS and Debian, user accounting is in `/var/log/lastlog`, while FreeBSD puts it in `/var/log/utx.lastlogin`. It also prints the welcome message when the user logs in, informing them of the last time they logged in.

Pam_lastlog only works as part of a session statement.

Linux-PAM supports several options to modify pam_lastlog's accounting and login behavior. You can disable certain accounting functions with options like *nowtmp* and *noupdate*. Options like *noterm* and *nohost* remove information from the user's login message, while *showfailed* displays the last time someone failed to log into this account. Finally, the *inactive* option lets you set a number of inactive days before the account is locked out for inactivity. You can set a number of days, or use the default of 90.

```
session  optional  pam_lastlog.so showfailed inactive=5
```

BSD systems handle all of these functions elsewhere, so OpenPAM supports none of these features.

Preventing Logins

No matter how far in advance you announce a maintenance window, and how many times you remind people, someone will try to use the system when you're doing a delicate upgrade. You might want to have a system in multi-user mode but disallow anyone except sysadmins from logging in. Or you might need to solve an administrative problem by not letting people log in for a while. The *pam_nologin* module is just for you.

You might think you can achieve similar results by turning services off—nobody can log into your host via SSH if the SSH daemon is off! You could also reconfigure SSH to allow only sysadmins to log in, but touching configuration files has its own risks. The pam_nologin module doesn't universally prohibit logins. It prohibits logins by everyone except a list of privileged users.

Pam_nologin checks for the existence of a `nologin` file—`/etc/nologin` or `/var/run/nologin` for Linux-PAM and OS X, and `/var/run/nologin` for OpenPAM. If the `nologin` file does not exist, users can log in normally. If the file exists, most users cannot log in. Pam_nologin uses the contents of the `nologin` file as an error message to the application. Whether or not the user sees that message depends entirely on the application.

Some systems remove the `nologin` file at boot, while others leave it in place at boot. What does your operating system do? Check the documentation to see what it claims, then try on a test host to discover what it really does.

Both OpenPAM and Linux-PAM recommend making pam_nologin a required module, and putting it at the front of a policy. Use it in every system service you intend to temporarily refuse access to.

Pam_nologin controls account availability, and works only in account policies. The account policy determines if an account is available.

When you have a `nologin` file using Linux-PAM, the **root** user can still log in. As **root** can't usually log in via SSH, this restricts logins to the console.

With OpenPAM, a `nologin` file restricts logins to users who have `ignorenologin` defined in `/etc/login.conf`. On FreeBSD this defaults to only **root**, but there's a commented-out example for a **staff** login class with this capability.

Now that you know something about the most pervasive modules, let's look at some of the internals PAM uses to hold everything together.

Chapter 3: PAM Items, Codes, and Functions

Much PAM documentation assumes that the sysadmin is familiar with the internal workings of PAM. The designers expect you to understand which functions PAM calls for each type of statement and which internal items and error codes PAM slings around. Configuring PAM modules and Linux-PAM extended controls requires understanding these return codes.

You don't need to memorize everything in this chapter. PAM items are critical in debugging, and you really do need familiarity with them. Specific PAM error codes and functions are less vital for sysadmins, however. Study the principles involved and what these codes are used *for*, but don't sweat the details of individual codes and functions. You can always look up an error code when a PAM module spits it out, and you'll quickly grow familiar with the errors bedeviling your environment.

PAM Items

PAM carries a whole bunch of its internal state in a set of well-defined *items*. A process that uses PAM defines the needed items and passes them off to the various PAM stacks. All of the items start off undefined. Applications and frameworks set the items they need. Modules read the items.

Modules make their decisions based on these items. I often find that modules use these items in unexpected ways. When authentication obstinately refuses to behave in the manner you expect, falling back to check these items and the module documentation is a great place to start.

Items can change as PAM runs through a policy. Applications can change these items as modules provide information. Some applications might forget critical authentication information when a module returns a specific code. Modules that return that code need to go at the end of the policy, after the decisions have been made. Applications might make up placeholder data for an item. Looking at the value of items is a good way to figure out why PAM has gone sideways under a program.

PAM items can contain security-sensitive information. For that reason I strongly recommend studying and experimenting with PAM items on a disposable virtual machine, rather than in your production environment. PAM uses items to include facts such as usernames, hostnames, passwords, and services. Not all PAM-aware programs define all items. Defining a remote host makes no sense for su(1), for example.

Here are the common PAM items.

PAM_SERVICE

The PAM_SERVICE item contains the name of the policy requested by the application. This is normally the name of the program that's calling PAM—something like `su`, `ftpd`, `sshd`, and so on. You could recompile a program to use a different service name, but that's not commonly done.

PAM_USER

You might think that PAM_USER would give the username of the user requesting authentication.

You'd be wrong.

PAM_USER is the username that something is trying to authenticate *to*. If you're logging on with FTP, for example, PAM_USER equals your FTP account. If you're running `su root`, however, you're trying to authenticate as **root**. PAM_USER therefore equals **root**.

PAM_RUSER

The item PAM_RUSER contains the requesting user. It might be a remote user. It could be the user requesting su(1) access. A module might set this to the same value as PAM_USER. It might not set this at all, if this application involves only a single user account.

PAM_TTY

See which terminal a process is running on by checking PAM_TTY. This might be a virtual terminal like `pts/2` or a console login like `tty2`. If this is a graphic application that doesn't really have a terminal, it could be the contents of the `$DISPLAY` environment variable.

PAM_HOST

This gives the hostname where the authentication is taking place. It's almost always the local host.

PAM_RHOST

The PAM_RHOST item gives the host where the client runs. For an application like FTP, it contains the client's hostname or IP address. Not all client-server applications set PAM_RHOST. Also, applications that run locally, like su(1), don't normally set PAM_RHOST.

PAM_CONV

This item contains a data structure for the PAM conversation the application expects. A sysadmin who needs to dig through this is in trouble.

PAM_AUTHTOK

The authentication token is the user's current password, or password-like thing.

PAM_OLDAUTHTOK

This is the user's expired password. You'll see this when changing passwords.

PAM_USER_PROMPT

This contains the prompt used to request a username for authentication.

PAM_AUTHTOK_PROMPT

This item gives the prompt to request a password.

PAM_OLDAUTHTOK_PROMPT

This contains the prompt used to request an expired password. You'll see this when a user needs to change their password before logging in.

PAM_SM_FUNCTION

Linux-PAM added PAM_SM_FUNCTION to store which PAM service module function the module is called with. Most sysadmins won't need this, but don't let its sudden unexpected appearance disturb you.

PAM_TYPE

Linux-PAM also added PAM_TYPE to show the type of policy that called a module. This contains auth, account, password, or session. Linux-PAM calls almost always define PAM_TYPE.

I discuss PAM functions and service module functions later this chapter.

Reading Items with pam_exec

While PAM modules pass items around, they don't really provide an interface for displaying them to mere sysadmins. Linux-PAM systems offer pam_warn to dump information from PAM, but it's not universally available. We'll see pam_warn in Chapter 6. Every Unix-like system supports using the pam_exec module to copy debugging information out of a policy, however. Chapters 6 and 7 cover pam_exec in detail, but we'll touch on it here.

Pam_exec lets you run arbitrary commands as part of a policy. Most often, this is a shell script. (You can put simple commands directly into a pam_exec statement, but that feels more fragile to me.) We'll use a simple example to copy all PAM items from the policy into the system log. Almost every operating system includes pam_exec.

Here's a simple script for capturing PAM items and writing them to the system log. I install this as */usr/local/scripts/pamvarlog.sh*, but you can put it in your preferred location.

```sh
#!/bin/sh

set | grep PAM | xargs logger
```

This pulls all environment items, grabs any item or value that contains PAM, and sends them to the system log.

Now attach this script to the PAM policy for a service, preferably near the top. You don't want a requisite statement to prevent the script from running before you have your data.

```
auth       required    pam_exec.so /usr/local/scripts/pamvarlog.sh
account    required    pam_exec.so /usr/local/scripts/pamvarlog.sh
session    required    pam_exec.so /usr/local/scripts/pamvarlog.sh
password   required    pam_exec.so /usr/local/scripts/pamvarlog.sh
```

Add these statements to your test system's main auth policy: `/etc/pam.d/system` on FreeBSD, `/etc/pam.d/system-auth` on CentOS, and Debian's four `/etc/pam.d/common-` files. You'll get messages like this in `/var/log/messages`.

```
Mar  2 14:54:23 host1 mwl: PAM_RUSER=mwl PAM_SERVICE=su
PAM_TTY=pts/0 PAM_TYPE=auth PAM_USER=root
Mar  2 14:54:25 host1 mwl: PAM_RUSER=mwl PAM_SERVICE=su
PAM_TTY=pts/0 PAM_TYPE=account PAM_USER=root
```

This immediately shows that the user **mwl** ran su(1) on terminal `pts/0`, and the request hit both the auth and account policies. The script doesn't log the results of the `su` request, but most programs that use authentication can perform their own logging.

```
Mar  2 14:54:25 host1 su: (to root) mwl on pts/0
```

PAM modules often expect you to understand which items it uses. We'll see an example of this behavior in Chapter 5.

PAM Return Codes

Success and failure aren't always clearly delineated. Just as politics has a whole scale of gray between "yes, absolutely!" and "That's it, I'm moving to Canada/Russia/Antarctica/Discworld," PAM has a bunch of possible answers besides "yes" and "no." There's a shipping container of difference between "wrong password" and "the sysadmin configured this PAM module incorrectly," and neither is the same as "the LDAP server is down."

When PAM calls a module, the module responds with precisely one return code. The exact interpretation of that return code depends on that module—an "expired password" error means something different if you have passwords locally versus in LDAP.

54

PAM includes 30 return codes, numbered 0 to 29. Many of them crop up only in bizarre circumstances or when the system is misconfigured. Mismatched binary types and un-loadable libraries show up in the system log, and are familiar if annoying parts of every sysadmin's troubleshooting routine. For the complete list, check out the X/Open Single Sign-on Service (XSSO) Pluggable Authentication Modules specification or pam(3).

Each return code has a formal name, usually given in all caps, starting with PAM. You'll see return codes like PAM_SUCCESS, PAM_AUTH_ERR, and so on. You might see the return code number, from 0 to 29. You might also see the return code name in lower case, without the leading PAM_. That is, return codes *PAM_SUCCESS*, *0*, and *success* all refer to the same thing.

Many return codes appear to overlap. To a system programmer they don't, but for a sysadmin they do. Return codes like PAM_CRED_EXPIRED and PAM_AUTHTOK_EXPIRED mean that the authentication credentials or password expired. Which error you get depends on how you're authenticating, but for a sysadmin, they both mean that the user's password or other authentication token is no longer valid.

You don't need to know every PAM return code. You do need to know that the return codes exist, that each PAM call returns one and only one code, and how to learn more about each code when it appears.

Here are the PAM return codes you're most likely to encounter.

PAM_SUCCESS (0)

The request fully succeeded. The user authenticated correctly. This is an unqualified yes.

PAM_SERVICE_ERR (3)

Some service that the PAM module needs has failed you. This appears most commonly with centralized authentication, when the Kerberos, LDAP, or NIS servers have gone belly-up.

PAM_SYSTEM_ERR (4)

The module experienced an OS-level error when trying to run.

PAM_PERM_DENIED (7)

The module says that this user lacks the privileges needed to return success. This permission error could be anywhere in the application stack. Check your system log.

PAM_MAXTRIES (8)

The module has a limit on the maximum number of times you can try to enter the correct authentication credentials. You've blown past that.

PAM_AUTH_ERR (9)

An error in authentication has occured. The user entered the wrong password.

PAM_NEW_AUTHTOK_REQD (10)

Most frequently, getting this return code means that the user's password has expired and must be changed. In PAM modules not related to passwords, however, it might appear when some password-like entity needs adjustment or replacement.

Only account policies should return this code.

PAM_USER_UNKNOWN (13)

The authentication system doesn't recognize this user.

PAM_IGNORE (25)

The PAM policy should ignore the result of this module, and not let it vote on allowing or denying access.

Functions

Each type of PAM request has well-defined programming interfaces to perform the task. These APIs both give PAM its flexibility and limit its scope. Sysadmins don't have to know how to use these functions, of course. If they appear in documentation or the system log, though, knowing roughly what the function does can help debug issues.

PAM Setup and Resources

Setting up a PAM session requires that a program call the *pam_start* function. When the PAM session completes, the *pam_end* function tears down the session and releases all the resources the session used.

A program's PAM session is a conversation between the program and the PAM libraries. A PAM application needs a "conversation callback," a way for the PAM stack to send messages back to the application, provided by the *pam_conv* function.

In addition to the items discussed earlier this chapter, PAM includes a whole list of internal items. Even the prompt presented to the user is an item. The *pam_set_item* and *pam_get_item* functions let PAM manipulate these items.

The *pam_setenv*, *pam_getenv*, *pam_putenv*, and *pam_getenvlist* functions allow PAM to manipulate the user environment before logging in. For example, a module like pam_krb5 would use these functions to set $KRB5CCNAME to the credential cache where it stored your ticket at login.

A PAM module might need to allocate memory for its own internal functions. While the PAM programming interface is strictly defined, a PAM module can do anything it likes internally. The *pam_set_data* and *pam_get_data* let a PAM session create and manipulate these chunks of memory by name.

Authentication Functions

As the name implies, the *pam_authenticate* function authenticates the user. The function takes the username and an authentication token (a password, fingerprint, gene scan result, or so on) and checks them against an authentication database.

The *pam_setcred* function manages a user's credentials. A user's credentials can include items like the user's username and group memberships, as well as things like Kerberos tickets or other single-sign-on accoutrements.

PAM modules do not set a user's UID or GID. Nor do they perform actions like opening a virtual terminal for the user. These actions normally need to be done by a child process. If a PAM module were to drop privileges from **root** to the user's when it called pam_setcred, the module would lose access to privileged operations like updating the lastlog. Instead, the server spawns a child process for the user's activity, while the server process maintains its privileges and cleans up after itself.

Account, Session, and Password Functions

PAM uses the *pam_acct_mgmt* function to enforce account policies. Any restrictions on logon hours, password expiration, or other account statements pass through pam_acct_mgmt.

Session statements trigger the *pam_open_session* and *pam_close_session* functions.

Finally, the *pam_chauthtok* function lets the server change the user's password.

PAM Service Functions

In addition to the functions used to call PAM, you'll see functions that PAM itself uses to call modules. These service module functions are how each module responds to a type of request. Each service module function corresponds to a regular PAM function, and starts with *pam_sm_* rather than just *pam_*.

The service module functions are *pam_sm_acct_mgmt*, *pam_sm_authenticate*, *pam_sm_chauthtok*, *pam_sm_close_session*, *pam_sm_open_session*, and *pam_sm_setcred*. So pam_sm_acct_mgmt is just like pam_acct_mgmt, but used within a module rather than PAM.

Why would you need to know all this? For one thing, Linux-PAM's extended controls make heavy use of PAM return codes.

Chapter 4: Linux-PAM Extended Controls and Substacks

PAM defines four common control statements: required, requisite, sufficient, and optional (as well as the widely-ignored binding). These controls determine how a PAM module's successes and failures affect a user's authentication.

Linux-PAM offers additional *extended control statements* that let you fine-tune responses, as well as the substack parameter that lets you divert policy processing. These appear only in Linux-PAM.

Extended Controls

A *yes* from a PAM module is always PAM_SUCCESS, but a *no* comes in endless flavors. Each PAM module might return one of several different responses to a query. With extended controls, you can fine-tune how a PAM statement handles rejection based on these responses.[10] Remember, a module returns one and only one response to each query.

Extended controls replace the four PAM controls with a specific instruction for each response a module might return, plus a generic catch-all instruction for any responses you don't specify. "If this module returns X, block access. If the module returns Y, that's good enough. If the module returns Z, immediately grant access. Any other answer, try the next module."

---

10   If only a human being's handling of rejection was so easily tuned!

Identify extended controls by using square brackets ([]) around them. Here's an example of an extended control from CentOS, for the module pam_securetty.

```
auth [user_unknown=ignore success=ok ignore=ignore \
    default=bad] pam_securetty.so
```

Each entry within the brackets represents a PAM response, with the leading PAM_ stripped off, in lower case. An equals sign separates the response from the instruction on how to handle that response. This entry says that when this module returns PAM_USER_UNKNOWN the policy should take the action "ignore." When the module returns PAM_SUCCESS, follow the action called "ok." If the response is PAM_IGNORE, take the action "ignore." The default instruction, used when the module responds with anything else, is "bad."

The pam_securetty manual page lists five possible response codes: PAM_SUCCESS, PAM_AUTH_ERR, PAM_INCOMPLETE, PAM_SERVICE_ERR, and PAM_USER_UNKNOWN. The extended control defines custom actions for PAM_SUCCESS and PAM_USER_UNKNOWN. All of the other cases tell PAM to take the action "bad."

Extended Control Actions

Consider PAM policies for a moment. Most statements in a policy affect the decision on whether or not to permit access. At any given point the policy might have a state like "allow access if nobody else objects" or "we're definitely rejecting the request, but you later modules can do your book-keeping." Linux-PAM's seven extended control actions are designed to alter the state of that policy.

The *bad* action tells PAM that the authentication request has failed. That's why our example above uses it as the default—we care about a couple specific failures, but for most failures, we just say "no." If the module reply triggers bad, it's as if a required module failed. PAM continues processing the policy, but authentication is ultimately rejected unless deliberately reset.

The *die* action tells PAM that the authentication request has failed, and that it must immediately stop processing the policy. Modules that follow this one will not get processed. When a reply triggers die, the PAM policy behaves as if a requisite module failed.

The *ok* action tells PAM that the authentication request was successful. Access is allowed, provided no other module objects. It's normally applied to the PAM_SUCCESS return code. An ok cannot override a bad response from elsewhere in the PAM policy. When a reply triggers ok, the PAM policy behaves like a required module succeeded.

The *done* action tells PAM that the authentication request was successful, and that PAM should immediately stop processing the policy. If nothing earlier in the policy returned bad, the policy permits access. When a reply triggers done, the PAM policy behaves like a sufficient module succeeded.

An *ignore* action indicates that this response doesn't alter the policy's response. An earlier bad or ok stands. The module can still carry out other actions, such as logging or running unrelated commands, but PAM doesn't let the results of the module's work or checks affect its decision on access. It's like the most common case of the optional control.

The *reset* action tells PAM to throw away any previous bad or ok results and keep processing the policy, getting a new success or failure from the remaining modules. It's unique to Linux-PAM. As with the binding control, I've never seen reset deployed in production.

Last, you can specify a number as an action. Triggering the number tells Linux-PAM to skip that many following modules in the policy. A number is most often used with the pam_succeed_if module, as discussed in Chapter 5.

Standard Controls in Extended Format

Each of the standard PAM controls can be expressed in the Linux-PAM extended control format. Understanding these can improve your understanding of both the extended controls and the traditional controls.

The required control can be expressed like so.

```
[success=ok new_authtok_reqd=ok ignore=ignore default=bad]
```

If the PAM module returns PAM_SUCCESS or PAM_NEW_AUTHTOK_REQD, this control takes the ok action. Authentication is successful. If the module returns PAM_IGNORE, PAM ignores the module. If the module returns anything else, the bad action is taken and authentication fails.

A requisite control looks very similar.

```
[success=ok new_authtok_reqd=ok ignore=ignore default=die]
```

The only difference between requisite and required is the default action. Where a required control defaults to bad, a requisite control defaults to die. If a module with this control fails, access is rejected and processing stops immediately.

Sufficient controls look entirely different.

```
[success=done new_authtok_reqd=done default=ignore]
```

If the module returns PAM_SUCCESS or PAM_NEW_AUTHTOK_REQD, the policy immediately permits access. Thanks to the done action, no further processing happens. Any other response doesn't affect the policy's voting, although the module might take other action on the system.

The optional control resembles sufficient.

```
[success=ok new_authtok_reqd=ok default=ignore]
```

Here, a PAM_SUCCESS or PAM_NEW_AUTHTOK_REQD gets this module to say ok and permit access. Any other result means that this module neither permits nor denies access. Processing continues, but other modules can still veto access.

Substacks

Linux-PAM supports processing detours, or *substacks*. While an include pulls the appropriate rules from that file into the PAM policy, PAM processes a substack separately. A control in a substack file can't make the whole policy stop processing—it can only terminate the substack and return to the main PAM policy. A decision made in a substack does affect the policy's decision to permit or deny access.

Let's walk through a common substack example. Here's the auth policy from CentOS' `/etc/pam.d/login`, which regulates console logins.

```
auth [user_unknown=ignore success=ok ignore=ignore \
     default=bad] pam_securetty.so
auth   substack   system-auth
auth   include    postlogin
```

This policy starts by checking the pam_securetty module (Chapter 2). It then drops into the substack contained in the file `system-auth`. Many CentOS PAM configurations use `system-auth` as a substack, permitting a common configuration across multiple services.

```
auth   required    pam_env.so
auth   sufficient  pam_fprintd.so
auth   sufficient  pam_unix.so nullok try_first_pass
auth   requisite   pam_succeed_if.so \
                   uid >= 1000 quiet_success
auth   required    pam_deny.so
```

Consider how this substack gets processed. The first module, pam_env (Chapter 5), is required. If this module fails, the request is rejected even if later modules return success. We then have two sufficient modules. Either one of these can return success and immediately terminate processing the substack. The fourth is requisite, meaning that if it's successful, policy processing immediately ends. The last module, pam_deny, always returns failure.

The substack has three control statements that can immediately terminate the auth policy—two required and a requisite. If any of these trigger in the substack, though, processing immediately returns to the main policy. Maybe the substack approved access, or maybe it rejected access. In any case, no matter what the substack declares, PAM processes the rest of the main part of the policy.

Go back to `/etc/pam.d/login` policy. No matter how the `system-auth` substack ends, PAM includes the `postlogin` file and processes those statements. As that's an include rather than a substack, statements in the include file can terminate the policy early.

This takes you through the Linux-PAM extensions to PAM. Now let's look at some popular Linux-PAM modules.

Chapter 5: Popular Linux-PAM Modules

While Linux-PAM copied a whole bunch of ideas from the primordial Solaris PAM, it's evolved in the last two decades. Developers have added new features, separated functions into different modules, and added support for every new hardware device they could get their mitts on.

This chapter discusses a few modules that are both exclusive to Linux-PAM and widely used in Debian or CentOS.

Popular OpenPAM Modules

Why dedicate a chapter to Linux-PAM modules and not give equal treatment to OpenPAM modules?

Many of the features Linux-PAM implements are not needed on typical (BSD) OpenPAM systems. BSD systems had features like user resource limits years before PAM or even Linux were created, and so don't implement those features in PAM. And BSD systems don't need `systemd`, so there's no need for pam_systemd.

Most OpenPAM-based systems ship with modules not found in default Linux-PAM setups, such as pam_ssh. These modules are available as add-ons to Linux-PAM, however. We cover many of them separately through the latter part of this book.

User Environment: pam_env

PAM lets the system manipulate a user's environment before the environment really exists. You can use pam_env to assign variables in the user environment before the user's own shell files are read. You can use pam_env in auth or session statements.

The pam_env module pulls its settings from the pam_env-specific configuration file, the system environment file, and the user's environment files.

pam_env Configuration

The primary pam_env configuration file, `/etc/security/pam_env.conf`, lets you set environment variables that vary depending on how the user connects. You provide a default value, and then possibly a conditional alternative, or override, if desired. The rules have this general format.

```
variable  default  override
```

If a statement has no override, pam_env sets the environment variable for the user. Here we unconditionally set the EDITOR variable.

```
EDITOR  pico
```

A user can override this setting with the usual shell configuration, but this lets you set a reasonable default.

If this was all pam_env let you do, it'd be pretty lame. But pam_env also lets the system make decisions based on the PAM environment. PAM sets its own variables, and a connecting user probably brings part of their own environment along. Look at the following example.

```
REMOTEHOST  DEFAULT=localhost  OVERRIDE=@{PAM_RHOST}
```

The default value of $REMOTEHOST is **localhost**. If nothing else, assume that the user connected from the local machine. An override is available, though. If the PAM item PAM_RHOST exists, we set $REMOTEHOST to that value instead. The @{} syntax indicates pam_env should check for a PAM item.

You might want to rely on user environment variables instead, such as $SSH_CLIENT or $DISPLAY. Use ${} to check for a user environment variable.

```
DISPLAY  DEFAULT=${REMOTEHOST}:0.0  OVERRIDE=${DISPLAY}
```

Earlier in *pam_env.conf*, we assigned the user a $REMOTEHOST environment variable. Here we use that to help assign a sensible value to $DISPLAY. If the user brought along their own $DISPLAY, however, let them keep it.

You can set an alternative PAM configuration file with the *conffile* option. This lets you set up different environments for different services. You might want a special environment for FTP users, and could set it in */etc/pam.d/ftpd* like so.

```
session   required   pam_env.so \
          conffile=/etc/security/pam_env_ftpd.conf
```

The default *pam_env.conf* has no uncommented entries.

System Environment

You can use the system environment file, */etc/environment*, to unconditionally hammer variables into the user's environment. Unlike shell-specific files like */etc/bash.bashrc*, */etc/environment* affects all users regardless of their shell.

Unlike *pam_env.conf*, */etc/environment* is not interpreted at all. If you want interpolation and decision-making, use *pam_env.conf* instead. Each line contains a variable name, an equals sign, and the value, like below.

```
IRCSERVER=irc.mwl.io
```

Further entries cannot refer back to the value of $IRCSERVER. An entry like the below sets the variable $BABBLE to the literal string $IRCSERVER rather than irc.mwl.io.

```
BABBLE=$IRCSERVER
```

The user's shell interprets these values, and can overwrite them.

Pam_env uses the flag *readenv* to control reading `/etc/environment`. By default, pam_env reads and uses the environment file. Set readenv to 0 to disable reading the environment.

```
session   required   pam_env.so readenv=0
```

You can also set a different environment file with the *envfile* flag, an equals sign (=), and the full path to an environment file. This lets you set different environments for different services.

User Environments

Users can have their own environment files, and you can have pam_env read and impose those environment files at boot. This is rarely a good idea, but sometimes it's the only idea. The *userenv* pam_env flag lets you set a file containing desired environment variables. This file is relative to the user's home directory. Set the *user_readenv* flag to 1 to enable this functionality.

Use userenv only if a particular user's environment must be set early in the login process, and you can't set that environment for all users.

The user environment file works exactly like the system environment file.

pam_env and Security

PAM modules can use the user's environment and PAM items to make decisions. By invoking pam_env, you're feeding new variables into the PAM authentication or session policy. It's possible that an environment variable set by pam_env could change the results of a PAM decision.

The risk increases if you allow the use of user environment files. While PAM modules are usually carefully programmed, I'm very reluctant to declare that a user environment file cannot subvert the authentication process. Users are clever. If you permit user environment files, pay close attention to your system security and behavior.

While the pam_env manual page declares that pam_env should appear last in any policy, to minimize the risk of environment contamination affecting authentication or session configuration, this advice has resulted in security flaws such as CVE-2010-4708 and CVE-2011-3149. Both CentOS and Debian put pam_env first in policies to minimize risks.

I recommend avoiding pam_env if possible.

Conditional Success: pam_succeed_if

Linux-PAM's *pam_succeed_if* module lets you perform a wide variety of checks based on user account settings, the service being checked, and the connection. You can compare any of these characteristics to values you choose.

At the user level, pam_succeed_if lets you check the username (user), UID (uid), GID (gid), shell, and home directory (home). If PAM sets the ruser or rhost items, you can check those. Finally, you can check the terminal (tty) or service.

You can compare these as numbers, strings, and list members. Additionally, you can do basic user group membership comparisons, much like pam_wheel. If a comparison matches, the module succeeds. If the comparison doesn't match, the module fails.

String Comparisons

You can compare just about anything as a string. Even numbers can be strings, but that's rather limited except for precise matches. Pam_succeed_if lets you do exact string comparisons with the equals sign (=). You can see if an item doesn't match a string with the != operator.

Additionally, you can use globs, or shell-style regular expressions. The =~ operator succeeds if an item matches a glob, and !~ succeeds if the item doesn't match the glob.

Here's a Debian configuration for prohibiting **root** from logging on with GDM.

```
auth  required  pam_succeed_if.so user != root quiet_success
```

If the user does not equal the string *root*, pam_succeed_if returns success.

Numerical Comparisons

You can compare the UID and GID to numbers. These are most useful for defined application accounts with constant user and group ID numbers, like **www** and **tcpdump** and the like. Use the standard mathematical operators for less than ($<$), less than or equal to ($<=$), greater than ($>$), greater than or equal to ($>=$). Pam_success_if uses the equals sign and the $!=$ notation in string comparisons; instead, use eq for equals and ne for not equal.

CentOS uses pam_succeed_if in the system-wide defaults, */etc/pam.d/system-auth*, to prevent user accounts with a UID less than 1000 from authenticating.

```
auth  requisite  pam_succeed_if.so \
      uid >= 1000 quiet_success
```

CentOS reserves UIDs of 1000 and below for application accounts. User accounts start with UID 1000. An account with a UID below 1000 should never authenticate. While most of these accounts block interactive use by using */sbin/nologin* as their shell, PAM adds another layer of protection.

The *quiet_success* option here tells pam_succeed_if to not brag about passing this test.

List Comparisons

To compare an item with a list, pam_succeed_if offers the *in* and *notin* operators. Give the list of comparisons after the operator, separated by colons, much like this.

```
thing notin item1:item2:item3
```

You might disallow a user from authenticating to a service by using such a list.

```
auth  required  pam_succeed_if user notin mwl:jkh:des
```

So long as the user is not **mwl**, **jkh**, or **des**, the module succeeds.

Debian uses extended permissions to control PAM on a per-service basis. We'll see an example of that in Chapter 10.

User Group Membership

You can use pam_succeed_if to check and see if a user is a member of a group or not. The *ingroup* operator returns success if the user is in the group, while *notingroup* succeeds if the user is not in the group. Here, we see if a user belongs to the group **customers**.

```
auth  sufficient  pam_succeed_if.so \
                   user ingroup customers
```

Similarly, the *innetgr* operator checks for NIS netgroup membership, while *notinnetgr* returns success if the user is not in the netgroup.

Conditional Rule Processing

Linux-PAM lets you skip statements in a PAM policy, as discussed in Chapter 4. This is mostly used with pam_succeed_if, creating PAM rules like "If this is true, skip the next rule in the policy." CentOS makes heavy use of this feature configuration with statements like this.

```
session   [success=1 default=ignore] pam_succeed_if.so \
                  service in crond quiet use_uid
session   required   pam_unix.so
```

We use Linux-PAM extended controls here to say that if pam_succeed_if returns PAM_SUCCESS, skip one rule. For any other result, ignore this module. Pam_succeed_if returns success if the service is crond. If the service is crond, we skip one line.

For any service other than crond, the PAM policy requires the pam_unix module.

Pam_succeed_if Options

In addition to the standard debug, pam_succeed_if has a couple special options.

The *use_uid* option tells PAM to check conditions using the requesting user's information, rather than the target user's. It switches the module from using PAM_USER to PAM_RUSER.

The *quiet* option tells the module to not log successes or failures to syslog. You can selectively silence only successes or failures with *quiet_success* and *quiet_fail*.

Finally, *audit* logs whenever someone checks for nonexistent users.

Local Users

In organizations with distributed user management, identifying users with local system accounts can be a useful part of an authentication system. The *pam_localuser* module returns success only if an account exists in the system's password file.

Note that pam_localuser doesn't actually check the user's local password; it only determines if the account exists. I've seen pam_localuser used in environments where the local accounts are for use only during complete LDAP failure. The mere presence of a local account, however, means that the user is permitted to use su(1) or sudo(1).

You can use an alternative password file with pam_localuser. Use the *file* option, an equals sign, and the path to the file.

Limiting User Resources: pam_limits

Linux-PAM can impose system resource constraints on users. System resources are no longer the scarce commodity they once were, but even now a user might start a process that consumes the entire CPU or fills up the host's memory. Resource limits help prevent these problems. You can impose resource limits with *pam_limits*.

Users running `bash` can view their limits with `ulimit`, while csh-based shells use `limit`.

Older Linux versions set these limits in `/etc/limits.conf`. Open-PAM systems normally handle this issue via login classes, outside of authentication.

Limits belong in the session PAM type.

The pam_limits system has two components, the PAM module itself and the limits files. While you can point pam_limits at any file you like, the default configuration file is `/etc/security/limits.conf`. Additional limits files go in the directory `/etc/security/limits.d`. Each line in `limits.conf` has four fields: a domain, a type, an item, and a value, much as shown here.

```
ftp  hard  nproc  0
```

The *domain* identifies which users this limit applies to. You can set limits by users, groups, wildcards, and ranges of UID and GID. In our example, the domain is the user **ftp**.

The *type* indicates if this is a hard or soft limit. Users can override soft limits, while hard limits are inviolate. Our example is a hard limit.

The *item* keyword defines which resource to limit. Pam_limits includes many resource keywords, which we'll discuss later. The example uses the item `nproc`, the keyword for the maximum number of processes.

The final field gives the maximum value for that resource.

The example above restricts user **ftp** to a maximum of zero processes. Hopefully that's an account used for the FTP service; otherwise, user Frederic Thomas Powell is going to be rather annoyed.

Limit Domains

You can identify users to be limited by username, group, UID, GID, or wildcard.

For limits that apply to a single username, use the username as the domain.

To use a system group put an @ symbol before the group name, such as @wheel, @staff, or @customers.

An asterisk (*) means that this limit applies to all users. "All users" does not include **root**, as the almighty **root** account is not bound by mortal chains. If you want a limit to apply to **root**, you must explicitly list **root** as the domain.

Pam_limits uses % as a special wildcard, specifically reserved for the *maxlogins* and *maxsyslogins* limits. Used alone, it sets a maximum number of non-**root** logins on this host. Put a group name after it to set a maximum number of logins for that group.

Specify a single UID with a leading colon, as shown here.

:1000

For a range of UIDs, give the lowest and highest matching UIDs, separated by a colon. Here we set limits on all users with UIDs from 1000 to 2000.

1000:2000

If you don't put a maximum matching UID, the limit applies to all UIDs equal to or greater than the one listed. Here we apply a limit to all UIDs 1000 and higher.

1000:

Group IDs work much like UIDs, except they have an @ symbol in front of them. Specify ranges with a colon. If you're matching a range of UIDs, PAM compares the user's primary group to the range. If you're matching a specific group, however, PAM looks at all groups the user belongs to. Here we impose a limit if the user is in GID 10000, even if it's not the user's primary group.

@:10000

Combine the % maxlogins-only wildcard with the group @ wildcard to limit the total number of logins of all users that are in the group. Here, if you're in group 10000, even if that's not your primary group, you're in the limited logins group.

%@:10000

Now decide what kind of limit this is.

Limit Type

Linux-PAM supports two kinds of limits, hard and soft.

A soft limit is a limit the user can raise. It's the operating system's way of saying "Hey, do you really want to use more than your share of resources?" The user can raise this limit with shell built-ins like `ulimit` or `limit`.

A hard limit is an absolute upper cap enforced by the kernel. The user cannot evade this limit.

Which should you use? Most users won't know how to evade a soft limit, so it's effectively a hard limit. Use both soft and hard limits if you have educated users. I normally use limits to restrict service accounts, to prevent web servers and databases from spiraling out of control. Hard limits are best in such cases—if my web server raises its own limits, I have a whole new set of problems…

Limit Items and Values

Linux-PAM can set limits on files, memory, processes, and logins. We won't cover exactly what all of these limits mean, as explaining things like stack size, locked memory, and so on would take another whole book.[11]

Most limits values are numerical. A user can open 100 files, or use a gigabyte of RAM, and so on. The exception is the word `unlimited`, which removes any limit on that user.

To set a maximum size on the user's core files, use the *core* limit. Setting `core` prevents an amok process from writing a multi-gigabyte core file when it finally screams and dies. To set a maximum size of a file the user can create, use the *fsize* limit. Both `core` and `fsize` take a value in kilobytes. Here we allow users with the primary group of **customers** to create 1 MB core files.

```
@customers  hard  core  1024
```

You can also limit the number of files the user can have open simultaneously, with *nofile*. To limit how many files the user can lock, use *locks*. Below, users in the **customers** group can only have 4096 files open simultaneously.

```
@customers  hard  nofile  4096
```

The four main memory restrictions are data, memlock, stack, and as. All are set in kilobytes. The *data* limit caps the amount of data the user can have in memory. The *memlock* value is the maximum amount of memory the user can have locked into memory. The *stack* limit sets a maximum stack size, while you can set an address space limit with *as*.

---

11   If you don't know what a knob does, don't twiddle it. In production.

You can limit the maximum amount of memory the user can claim for POSIX message queues with the *msgqueue* limit. Unlike other memory limits, msgqueue is in bytes.

The main ways to limit processor resources are by the number of concurrent processes and the total amount of CPU time. The *nproc* item lets you set a maximum number of simultaneous processes, while *cpu* lets you set a maximum CPU time in minutes. Here's how CentOS lets all system users have a generous 4,096 simultaneous processes, but explicitly removes any restrictions from **root**.

```
*       soft   nproc   4096
root    soft   nproc   unlimited
```

Another way to limit processor resources is to control how aggressively the operating system schedules the user's processes. The *priority* item lets you set the default niceness of the user's processes, as per nice(1). Higher values get less priority. Similarly, the *nice* item lets you set the maximum niceness available to the user. Using priority is a nice (no pun intended) way to let the user have resources when they're available, but shunt them aside when the system is loaded. Here, we tell the user **mwl** that his tasks don't matter.

```
mwl   soft   priority   10
```

If you're doing real-time computing, the *rtprio* item lets you set a user's real-time priority.

The *sigpending* item lets you limit the number of signals a user can have pending. The worrisome thing about this setting is that it was written because someone needed it.

Restrict the total number of simultaneous system logins a user or group can have with the *maxlogins* option. If you want to restrict the total number of non-**root** logins on the system, use the *maxsyslogins* option. Here we limit the user **mwl** to two simultaneous logins.

```
mw1   hard   maxlogins   2
```

Remember, when limiting the number of logins by group membership, you'll need to use the special % wildcard discussed in "Limit Domains," above.

Finally, the *chroot* limit lets you define a directory to chroot(8) a user into. In most cases you wouldn't use pam_limits to chroot a user, instead relying on server software such as sshd(8).

PAM and Systemd

What does authentication have to do with systemd(8)?

Systemd does not authenticate users. PAM needs to notify systemd when each user logs in. Pam_systemd handles that communication. As systemd is not yet a mandatory component of most Linux systems, pam_systemd is usually an optional module. It goes at the end of the session policy.

The main function of pam_systemd is to manage systemd scopes and XDG base directories. Very few people need to adjust either of these, but you should know it's possible. See the systemd(8) manual page for details if you're one of those unfortunate few.

This takes you through the most commonly used Linux-PAM modules. Now let's talk about some generic PAM debugging.

Chapter 6: PAM Debugging

So you've carefully tuned your PAM statements, but it doesn't work as you expected. Maybe authentication dies somewhere for no discernible reason, or a desired module doesn't seem to get called at all. How can you tell which PAM modules get called, and when an authentication request dies?

In anything to do with computers, all debugging eventually falls back to some sort of `print` statement. PAM skips the preliminaries and drops you straight there. You can track a PAM request's progress through each policy with the system log, pam_echo, and pam_exec. You can also fire up program debuggers like ktrace(1) and truss(1).

There's nothing *quite* like that lovely feeling you get when you break a host's PAM configuration and no longer have **root** privileges to repair your error. Any time you adjust with a host's PAM configuration, make sure that you leave a terminal with **root** access open. Test all changes thoroughly. Make sure you can still get **root** access from a brand new session before logging out.

Any of these techniques can make the system leak authentication information into the system log or terminal sessions. I strongly recommend performing tests on a disposable virtual machine rather than on a system with live users.

PAM Logging

If you can't figure out why a module is behaving unexpectedly, start with logging.

Basic systems administration problems show up in the system log. My most common configuration file error, even after decades of shouting truly vile obscenities at PAM, is forgetting the .so at the end of a PAM module name. PAM searches for the nonexistent file *pam_unix* rather than *pam_unix.so*, the statement fails, and the policy denies access. These errors show up in system logs, usually in logs visible only to **root**. Check for these logged errors first.

PAM modules perform routine logging via syslog(3), with the facility auth. These normally wind up in a restricted log file accessible only to **root**, like */var/log/secure* on CentOS or */var/log/auth.log* on FreeBSD and Debian.

Many modules accept the *debug* argument to make the module more verbose. The contents and amount of information depend entirely on the module. PAM module developers all choose to log different things, even—or especially—with debugging turned on, so some PAM modules provide better debugging output than others.

But sometimes, you don't even get to the module...

Debugging with pam_echo

The pam_echo module prints stuff to the authenticating user. Not all programs pass these messages back to the user, but when it works it's enlightening and easy.

Using pam_echo

Pam_echo takes a string of text as an argument, the message to be passed back.

```
auth  optional  pam_echo PAM auth policy starting
```

If the application passes PAM messages back to the user, the text `PAM auth policy starting` will appear when the policy hits this statement.

Here's `/etc/pam.d/system` from a recent FreeBSD system. (I'm using FreeBSD here because the system auth policy is far shorter than an average Linux.) I've added a call to pam_echo before each module.

```
auth   required    pam_echo checking OPIE
auth   sufficient  pam_opie.so  no_warn no_fake_prompts
auth   required    pam_echo checking opieaccess
auth   requisite   pam_opieaccess.so  no_warn allow_local
auth   required    pam_echo checking UNIX auth
auth   required    pam_unix.so  no_warn try_first_pass nullok
```

When the user attempts to authenticate with a program like su(1), she'll get the pam_echo messages.

```
$ su -m
checking OPIE
checking opieaccess
checking UNIX auth
Password:
```

While this is noisy, we know that the auth request made it all the way to the end of the policy. It might also screw up shell scripts that aren't expecting the extra output. If an automated process starts spewing errors right about the time you put debugging echoes in, you know what happened.

pam_echo Items

You can display the contents of PAM items by using escape characters in a pam_echo statement. Pam_echo escape sequences are the % character, followed by a single letter.

%U is the requesting username, or PAM_RUSER.

%u is the target account's name, or PAM_USER.

%t is the terminal, or PAM_TTY.

%s is the service name, PAM_SERVICE.

`%H` is the host where the client is running, or PAM_RHOST.

Linux-PAM also supports `%h`, the local host.

Use these to spit out PAM internal items like so.

```
auth   required   pam_echo checking UNIX auth RUSER=%U \
                  USER=%u TTY=%t SERVICE=%s RHOST=%H
```

One problem with these items is that any two-character string beginning with a percent sign gets the percent sign stripped away. A percent sign is not a typical character in usernames, hostnames, and service names, but should you be one of the special few, be aware of this.

Linux-PAM Message Files

Linux-PAM lets you provide text to pam_echo through a separate text file. Use the *file=* option and a filename, like so.

```
auth   optional   pam_echo.so file=/etc/message
```

When the user authenticates, the text in `/etc/message` gets passed back to her. Adding this sort of configuration to your authentication process lets you add generic legal warnings to your system. You can use pam_echo items in the text file, much like this.[12]

```
Your access to this host as %u has been logged.
Unauthorized users will be mercilessly
trampled by angry Luggage.
```

This won't necessarily work for all services—remember, some programs don't hand this text back to the user. But it will handle many cases for you, and programs that don't pass the text back to the user often have a separate method for displaying these messages.

If pam_echo doesn't have access to everything you need, or if the client program won't return its output, try using pam_exec to extract more information from the PAM policy.

---

12   You should get better text than this, though. Perhaps even from a lawyer, or at least someone who plays one on TV.

Debugging with pam_exec

If the software you're debugging won't pass pam_echo messages through to the user, or if pam_echo doesn't have access to values you want to check, fall back on pam_exec.

We used pam_exec in Chapter 3 to capture a PAM session's environment variables. Chapter 7 covers pam_exec in more detail. Right now, we'll use it to send information about a PAM session to the system log. Here, pam_exec calls the script *pamdebug.sh*, giving the script an argument of the module that's about to be called.

```
auth   optional    pam_exec.so /usr/local/scripts/pamdebug.sh pam_opie
auth   sufficient  pam_opie.so            no_warn no_fake_prompts
auth   optional    pam_exec.so /usr/local/scripts/pamdebug.sh
                               pam_opieaccess
auth   requisite   pam_opieaccess.so     no_warn allow_local
auth   optional    pam_exec.so /usr/local/scripts/pamdebug.sh pam_unix
auth   required    pam_unix.so  no_warn try_first_pass nullok
```

The *pamdebug.sh* script logs what's about to be called.

```
#!/bin/sh
logger "process $PPID calling $1"
```

You could also add any other debugging you like to this script, such as capturing internal PAM variables. But as-is, the script creates log messages resembling this.

```
Mar 14 08:52:21 testhost mwl: process 1314 calling pam_opie
```

You've captured the user, the process ID, and the module called. With this information, you can sort out where your policy stopped processing, then use module-specific features to determine how that statement failed.

Debugging with pam_warn

Many Linux distributions offer *pam_warn* for debugging. The pam_warn module does not affect the authentication process, but sends the service, terminal, user, remote user, and remote host to the system log. Add pam_warn to the beginning of any auth policy you want to debug. Here I want to use pam_warn to debug su(1) on CentOS.

```
auth    optional      pam_warn.so
auth    sufficient    pam_rootok.so
auth    substack      system-auth
auth    include       postlogin
```

As pam_warn always returns PAM_IGNORE, you can use an optional or required control.

When a user tries to use su(1), each module in the policy sends messages to the system log.

```
Aug  2 00:52:39 centos su: pam_warn(su-1:auth): func-
tion=[pam_sm_authenticate] flags=0 service=[su-1] termi-
nal=[pts/3] user=[root] ruser=[mwl] rhost=[<unknown>]
Aug  2 00:52:41 centos su: pam_warn(su-1:setcred): func-
tion=[pam_sm_setcred] flags=0x2 service=[su-1] termi-
nal=[pts/3] user=[root] ruser=[mwl] rhost=[<unknown>]
Aug  2 00:52:41 centos su: pam_systemd(su-1:session):
Cannot create session: Already running in a session
Aug  2 00:52:41 centos su: pam_unix(su-1:session): ses-
sion opened for user root by (uid=500)
```

If you need to debug further, you might look at pam_debug to specifically set values in a PAM policy.

Between pam_warn, pam_exec, pam_echo, and the system log, you can extract almost any information from PAM. If one method doesn't work, try another. You'll need that flexibility for the next chapter...

Chapter 7: Arbitrary Files and Random Programs

The Unix model of group membership has limits. If your environment uses cross-platform NFS, for example, a single user can be a member of only 16 groups. You might want to delegate managing a group to a particular user, but most Unix-like systems don't give you that capability. (Solaris' capabilities system comes close.) Sometimes, you want PAM to just read a list of users that are allowed to access a service.

Similarly, you might want the login process to run a program as part of a PAM process. This might be part of an NIS configuration, or related to your firewall, or a component of your custom application.

You can use PAM modules for both of these. We'll start with Linux-PAM's pam_listfile.

Checking Files: pam_listfile

Traditional Unix systems included per-application lists of permitted or prohibited users. The classic example is `/etc/ftpusers`, which listed users forbidden to use FTP. If you tried to use FTP as, say, **root** or **operator**, the FTP daemon checked this file and kicked you out.

Linux-PAM's *pam_listfile* tells PAM to read a text file containing a list, and permit or reject access based on that list. You can permit or deny access based on the username or group, but also on the terminal device, the remote host or remote user, or the shell.

A typical use of pam_listfile looks like this.

```
auth   required   pam_listfile.so item=user sense=deny \
                  file=/etc/ftpusers onerr=succeed
```

This is part of the auth policy. We set this example to be required, but it could sensibly be requisite or sufficient. (Making a pam_listfile configuration optional would be kind of weird, but I'm not going to say it would never be appropriate.)

The *item* is what you're looking for in the list. In this case, we're checking the username. You can check shells, terminals, and more.

The *sense* is how pam_listfile should respond if an item is in the file. Here, we tell pam_listfile to deny the request if the username is in the file.

Pam_listfile needs to know the *file* to check.

Finally, we say how pam_listfile should behave if it has an unexpected error, with the *onerr* setting. This isn't an error like "the user isn't in the file," but rather "the file is unreadable" or "the kernel told me to bug off." Here, we tell pam_listfile to return success if it has an error.

This example implements the traditional `/etc/ftpusers` functionality. A username listed in the file may not authenticate to this service.

Let's look at each part of this separately.

Pam_listfile Items

While the username is the most obvious way to permit or block access, pam_listfile permits other options.

You might want to allow or deny access based on if the user is at the console or not. While there's a pam_console module, it configures the environment for console users. In most organizations, the only time you log onto the console is in a disaster. Suppose you want sysadmins to be able to run su(1) at the console, but when logging

on remotely they must use sudo(1) instead. Add an entry like this to
`/etc/pam.d/su`.

```
auth   required   pam_listfile.so item=tty sense=allow \
                  file=/etc/ttylist onerr=succeed
```

With a statement like this, pam_listfile compares the user's terminal (tty) to the file `/etc/ttylist`. If it finds a match, it returns the access given by the sense setting—in this case, `allow`.

The file `/etc/ttylist` needs to contain a list like this.

```
tty1
tty2
tty3
tty4
```

Blocking based on virtual terminals is more difficult. Linux creates virtual terminals as needed. You can't use wildcards or regular expressions in a pam_listfile file, so you'd need to list far more virtual terminals than you will ever actually have.

Allowing or blocking access based on the remote host can be done with the *rhost* item. As pam_listfile doesn't support any kind of wildcarding or netmasks, it's almost always the wrong place to perform such checks. If you absolutely must use remote host matching in PAM, use a file containing individual IP addresses and get ready for ongoing low-level annoyance.

You can allow or deny authentication based on the user's shell, as given in `/etc/passwd`. Here I deny authentication to all users who use a shell listed in `/etc/shelllist`.

```
auth   required   pam_listfile.so item=shell sense=deny \
                  file=/etc/shelllist onerr=succeed
```

Nothing stops a user from changing their shell, authenticating, and then restoring their preferred shell, however. You won't see shell-based block or permit lists very often.

Group membership is another criterion pam_listfile can process. It doesn't work quite the way you think, as discussed below, but here's an example.

```
auth  required  pam_listfile.so item=group sense=allow \
              file=/etc/grouplist onerr=succeed
```

If a user is a member of a group listed in /etc/grouplist, she gets access. If not, she doesn't.

Using pam_listfile with group membership is a great way to illustrate how PAM can ruin your whole day.[13] You might use a pam_wheel statement to only allow members of the **wheel** group to use a service, and then add a pam_listfile statement like the above to bar anyone in a group listed in /etc/grouplist from using that same service. Now add **wheel** to /etc/grouplist. You now have a completely valid PAM configuration that blocks everybody from authenticating.

Pam_listfile Sense and File

The *file* statement tells pam_listfile where to find the list of items it's looking for. Each item should be on its own line. As usual for configuration files, use a hash mark (#) to start a comment.

The *sense* statement tells pam_listfile what to do with the list. Setting sense to *allow* tells pam_listfile to only permit access to items listed in the file. Setting sense to *deny* blocks any items in the file.

Pam_listfile Errors

You break things, usually without intending to. The *onerr* statement tells pam_listfile what to do when it has a problem. Setting onerr to *succeed* tells pam_listfile to allow access if it has a problem. Setting onerr to *fail* causes it to fail shut, denying access.

---

13   To be fair, I can't blame pam_listfile. PAM has *many* ways to ruin your day.

No, "my username is not in the file" is not a PAM error. According to most people, the most common error is the absence of the list file[14]. Perhaps you want to allow access only to accounts listed in `/etc/access`. If that file is missing, should pam_listfile permit access? Or should it refuse? There is no universally correct answer, but onerr lets you choose your favorite failure mode.

Pam_listfile and Changing Usernames

You'll see weird behavior from pam_listfile when a user changes usernames, such as with su(1) or sudo(1). Pam_listfile checks access based on the target user, not the requesting user. It checks the PAM_USER item against the file, not PAM_RUSER.

Suppose you list user **mwl** in `/etc/access`, and configure su(1) to use pam_listfile to check for the username in `/etc/sulist` before permitting access. If user **mwl** runs `su root`, he will be denied access. In this case, **mwl** is the requesting user, not the target user. This means you could use pam_listfile to restrict which accounts someone may su(1) *to*, but not from.

Services like FTP don't change the username, however. There is no requesting user, only the user requesting authentication. Pam_listfile works well for these services. Alternatively, you could use pam_exec as discussed later.

OpenPAM versus pam_listfile

OpenPAM doesn't include pam_listfile. It's not even an available package for most BSD-based systems.

This might seem like an obvious missing piece, but parts get added to typical OpenPAM-based systems when they're needed. Nobody who's needed pam_listfile on an OpenPAM system has submitted a

---

14   According to me, the most common error is forgetting to put ".so" after the module name. The onerr flag doesn't help with that.

request to get it added. In part, this is because you can easily replicate pam_listfile by running a script. We'll look at that next.

Running Programs: pam_exec

As discussed in Chapters 3 and 6, PAM can run arbitrary commands with pam_exec. If the program runs successfully (returns 0), pam_exec returns success. If the program returns an error or fails to run at all, pam_exec returns failure.

Why would you use pam_exec? You might extract PAM environment items as discussed in Chapter 3. The textbook example is rebuilding the YP database after a user changes her password. But you can also use pam_exec to implement functions like checking a username against a list of users before permitting access, exactly like pam_listfile.

One thing to consider is that pam_exec fires up a process for each authentication request. If many people authenticate to your system, these processes can impose significant load. Verify that your "arbitrary commands" are not the metaphorical equivalent of hordes of kilt-wearing little blue men that think your system resources kebab up a treat.[15] Simple commands and scripts, however, should be fine for most environments.

Configuring pam_exec

It's possible to put commands directly in a PAM configuration file. For anything but the simplest commands, I find this fragile and easily broken. You might prefer otherwise, but as I'm the one writing this book, we'll do it my way. Instead, put the command you want PAM to execute in a script and have pam_exec call that script.

The simplest invocation of pam_exec takes only a single option, the command to run.

---

15   If pam_exec starts Firefox, you're doomed.

```
account   required   pam_exec /usr/local/scripts/pamvarlog.sh
```

When a user attempts to access their account, PAM runs the script *pamvarlog.sh*. We used this script in Chapter 3 to gather PAM environment variables.

OpenPAM and Linux-PAM both offer additional options to pam_exec, but we'll cover the basic functions first. Specifically, we'll implement a basic pam_listfile feature entirely through shell commands.

Implementing pam_listfile in pam_exec

We're going to have a list of users permitted access to a service. If the username exists in the file, access is granted. If not, access is denied.

PAM hands our script its usual batch of items. If you're not sure which items a particular server sets, capture them with the *pamvarlog.sh* script in Chapter 3. Fortunately, most every authentication process needs PAM_USER.

We need to be a little bit careful in how we check for the username in our target file. We don't want to match comments. We want to match only complete usernames. A little bit of grep(1) will do the trick for us. Here's a proof-of-concept script that checks the user against */etc/validusers*, and permits access if the username appears there.

```
#!/bin/sh
/usr/bin/grep ^$PAM_USER$ /etc/validusers
return $?
```

This script returns whatever the grep(1) statement returns. If grep(1) finds a match, it returns 0. If there's no match, it returns 1. Remember, pam_exec treats 0 as success and 1 as failure.

What if you want to deny access to users listed in */etc/bogususers*? That's a massive, intrusive change: add an exclamation point.

93

```
#!/bin/sh
! /usr/bin/grep ^$PAM_USER$ /etc/bogususers
return $?
```

This script inverts the return code of the grep(1) statement.

Build on these examples to create scripts that fit your needs. At a minimum, you *must* sanitize the inputs. The method for sanitizing inputs depends on your system's default root shell—bash has different methods than traditional sh.

Pam_exec versus Modules

Using pam_exec for everything seems like an easy and straightforward way to solve a lot of problems. We're sysadmins. We like shell scripts. "You want to authenticate against a NoSQL database? I'll write a shell script!"

Real life is not that simple.

When a PAM module exists for a function, you're usually better off using it as opposed to writing your own script. Obscure but publicly available PAM modules have probably had more users than your shell script. The worst bugs have already been found—and best of all, they've been found *by someone else*. If you write your own script, you get to find those bugs on your own.

Using pam_exec should be considered a last choice. It's a really useful last choice, though.

One thing to remember when using pam_exec is that Linux-PAM and OpenPAM implemented pam_exec differently.

OpenPAM pam_exec

OpenPAM's pam_exec has only one option, to adjust return codes.

OpenPAM's pam_exec in the default configuration returns one of two responses. If the command returns 0, pam_exec returns PAM_SUCCESS. If the command returns anything else, pam_exec returns PAM_PERM_DENIED.

The *return_prog_exit_status* option to pam_exec changes what it returns. Instead of a simple "yes" or "no," return_prog_exit_status lets the script return an actual PAM return code, as discussed in Chapter 4. Your script needs to return a valid return code for the service module function calling it. In Linux-PAM, you can check the PAM_SM_FUNC item to see the function calling pam_exec. The manual page for each service module function lists the acceptable return codes. Pam_exec knows which functions can accept which return codes. If your script tries to return an unacceptable code pam_exec substitutes PAM_SERVICE_ERR instead.

That's the only option OpenPAM pam_exec supports. While Linux-PAM's pam_exec supports more options, those options can almost all be implemented within a script.

Linux-PAM pam_exec

The Linux-PAM version of pam_exec has options for debugging, logging, and handling privilege and passwords.

The *debug* option sends debugging information to the system log, exactly as discussed in Chapter 1.

Your pam_exec command might generate output. That output is normally discarded, but you can use either the *log=* or *stdout* option instead. By defining a log file, you send any output to that file. The stdout option sends the program's output to standard out, letting the calling program deal with that output.

Even if the command doesn't normally generate output, pam_exec echoes any errors the program throws. The *quiet* option disables those messages.

The *type=* option tells pam_exec to run the command only if the PAM policy type matches. You could set, say, `type=account` so that this particular pam_exec only runs on account policies.[16]

You can hand your script the user's password on standard input, by adding the *expose_authtok* option. The system variable PAM_MAX_RESP_SIZE dictates the maximum password length, but that's normally something like 512 bytes.

Finally, you can run programs with the effective UID of the process being authenticated to, rather than the user being authenticated, by adding the *seteuid* flag.

PAM versus SELinux

Security Enhanced Linux, or SELinux, adds fine-grained access control to Linux systems. It commonly appears in CentOS-type systems. SELinux often prevents add-on PAM modules from functioning properly. The pam_ssh module, star of Chapter 10, is one of them, so we'll use it as an example.

Fixing SELinux-related problems involves verifying that SELinux is causing your problem, then adjusting the system security policy to permit this module to function.

Is It SELinux?

An SELinux-related error generally first appears as that "this really should work" feeling. If a program just won't run during login, or it almost works but some vital function crashes, check for an SELinux error.

Chapter 10 discusses using pam_ssh for workstation authentication. The pam_ssh module uses a user's SSH keys to authenticate to the

---

16   Theoretically, if you wanted a pam_exec statement to only apply to account requests, you could… not put the statement in your auth, session, and password policies? Or is that crazy talk?

local machine's console, starts the SSH agent `/usr/bin/ssh-agent`, and adds the SSH keys to the agent. (If you don't know what this means, grab a copy of *SSH Mastery* [Tilted Windmill Press, 2012]). You don't yet know about pam_ssh, but that doesn't matter for diagnosing its SELinux issues.

If you deploy pam_ssh on a recent version of CentOS, you'll be able to authenticate, but the module won't start an SSH agent. Add the debug flag to your pam_ssh statement and messages like these appear in `/var/log/secure`.

```
Jul  6 16:53:33 centos pam_ssh[3039]: exec /usr/bin/ssh-
agent
Jul  6 16:52:29 centos pam_ssh[3039]: /usr/bin/ssh-
agent: Permission denied
Jul  6 16:52:29 centos pam_ssh[3039]: /usr/bin/ssh-agent
exited with status 127
```

And yet, once you have a command prompt, you can run `ssh-agent` just fine.

It's inexplicable. It's senseless. Check for an SELinux problem.

While you can trawl through `/var/log/audit/audit.log` looking for `denied` statements, the most authoritative way to verify a problem comes from SELinux is to tell SELinux to log policy violations but not block them. This is called *permissive* mode. This is best done on a test system. Use setenforce(8) to switch enforcement modes.

```
# setenforce 0
```

Now try to log in again. With SELinux disabled, pam_ssh starts its SSH agent just fine. It's an SELinux issue. Turn SELinux back to *enforcing* mode.

```
# setenforce 1
```

The problem reappears. Yep, it's SELinux.

Now create an SELinux policy to permit this PAM module to function.

Creating an SELinux Policy

Before trying to change your system's SELinux policy, install the tools for SELinux management. On CentOS, the setroubleshoot package contains everything you need. We'll start with the `audit2allow` command that reads the audit log and creates policies.

Search the audit log to determine how SELinux is blocking the application. Here I'm searching for the keyword "denied" and the name of my PAM module, pam_ssh.

```
# grep denied audit.log | grep pam_ssh
```

If you don't get any results, try dropping the PAM module name. SELinux might be blocking a secondary process related to the module. When you do get results, though, feed them into `audit2allow`. Use `-m` and a module name to print the SELinux policy module proposal based on the error message.

```
# grep denied audit.log | grep pam_ssh | \
    audit2allow -m pam_ssh
module pam_ssh 1.0;

require {
  type unconfined_t;
  type ssh_agent_exec_t;
  class file entrypoint;
}

#============== unconfined_t ==============
allow unconfined_t ssh_agent_exec_t:file entrypoint;
```

Here comes the tricky part. Do you understand SELinux access control lists? If so, read the proposed policy and make sure it seems sensible. If not, either find someone with SELinux expertise and ask them to look, or decide to blindly trust `audit2allow`.

To create an actual SELinux policy on your system, use `audit2allow` with the -M flag and the actual module name. This only creates the policy; it does not activate it.

```
# grep denied audit.log | grep pam_ssh | audit2allow -M
pam_ssh
******************** IMPORTANT ***********************
To make this policy package active, execute:

semodule -i pam_ssh.pp
```

You're not one to ignore instructions, are you? Do what the nice software tells you.

```
# semodule -i pam_ssh.pp
```

Your PAM module should now work, or at least it should proceed to the next error. Which is progress, no?

Once you have a working SELinux policy, you can copy the *.pp* file containing the policy to other systems and install it. You must ensure that the SELinux policy version matches and that the types referenced in the policy exist in the other system. The best way to do this is to use the same operating system version for both your test and production environments.

SELinux and pam_mkhomedir

The pam_mkhomedir module creates missing home directories when the user logs in. It's used in organizations that deploy centralized authentication, such as LDAP. This book doesn't cover the module because it's very trivial.

One problem with pam_mkhomedir is that it doesn't support SELinux. Red Hat envisions SELinux as a core part of its operating system. Rather than update pam_mkhomedir, Red Hat has replaced pam_mkhomedir with the SELinux-friendly pam_oddjob_mkhomedir. A solution exists, so that's fine for most CentOS admins.

I've been in more than one multi-platform enterprise where the corporate security policy mandates use of pam_mkhomedir, however. Perhaps the security team hasn't updated its policy in a while. Perhaps this is part of a cross-platform standardization push. I've even seen a case of "dang it, the blasted sysadmins keep using pam_exec for *everything*!" Adjusting the SELinux security policy lets you use pam_mkhomedir on CentOS.

Eventually, you won't be able to get pam_mkhomedir on CentOS. Rather than adjusting the policy and going on with your day, talk to your security team. Find out what problem they're trying to solve. Help them either update the standard or solve their problem some other way.

But if you really want to play with your organization's security policy, you need add-on PAM modules.

Chapter 8: SSH Agent Authentication

Most sysadmins manage hosts with Secure Shell (SSH). The majority of SSH authentication happens with public keys rather than with passwords. If you're using an SSH agent, you can tell PAM to use the agent as an authentication source with the pam_ssh_agent_auth.

Pam_ssh_agent_auth (https://sourceforge.net/projects/pamsshagentauth/) works much the same as SSH key-based authentication. The module grabs the user's authorized_keys file and asks the user's SSH agent if it has the matching private key. If the SSH agent has the private key, the module returns PAM_SUCCESS. Pam_ssh_agent_auth is designed to authenticate sudo(1), so that's how we'll use it.

Authenticating against a user's SSH key is a kludgy knock-off of multi-factor authentication. It proves that the user has the key file and the passphrase to decrypt it. A key file is not a physical thing, of course. It can be copied and moved between machines. But it's slightly better than a plain password alone. For real two-factor authentication, you want something like Google Authenticator (Chapter 9) or invest in security tokens. On the other hand, SSH agent authentication lets you avoid ever typing a password on your servers.

Many organizations have legitimate reasons why they don't use SSH agents, or reasons why they don't want to authenticate programs in this manner. Compromising a user's SSH client can lead to server compromise. That's a valid objection in many environments. But pam_ssh_agent_auth is one of the simpler add-on PAM modules, so it's a good place to start exploring.

This module only works when your environment has a connection to an SSH agent. If you log in over a serial line, pam_ssh_agent_auth won't reach across the serial line onto your desktop and query your SSH agent. Even if you want to deploy pam_ssh_agent_auth everywhere, be sure you have alternate authentication methods for disaster recovery.

Installing pam_ssh_agent_auth

CentOS-based and FreeBSD systems offer a pam_ssh_agent_auth package. Debian has a pam-ssh-agent-auth package (as I write this, in the experimental repository).

If your operating system doesn't offer a package, download and compile it from the project page.

Configuring pam_ssh_agent_auth

All pam_ssh_agent_auth configuration takes place in the PAM configuration file. The biggest issue is finding the user's authorized_keys file, but you'll also have debugging and permissions options.

Locating authorized_keys

The *file* argument tells pam_ssh_agent_auth where to find the user's authorized_keys file. The simplest configuration points the module at the `authorized_keys` file in the user's home directory.

```
auth  sufficient  pam_ssh_agent_auth.so \
                file=~/.ssh/authorized_keys
```

The tilde character (~) expands to the user's home directory. You can also use `%h` to represent the user's home directory.

For more complicated setups, especially ones where you share PAM configurations across multiple hosts, you could use `%H` to represent the short hostname, `%u` to represent the username, or `%f` for the complete hostname. These come in more when centrally managing key files, as is common in many large-scale deployments. Configurations like this are very common.

```
auth  sufficient  pam_ssh_agent_auth.so \
                  file=/etc/ssh/keys/%u
```

Each user's public key file is named after their username, in the directory `/etc/ssh/keys`. My key file would thus be `/etc/ssh/keys/mwl`. Here the sysadmin team has a central configuration server, something like Ansible or Puppet, and distributes the keys to hundreds of servers with a single command. Users cannot update their `authorized_keys` files.

Some hosts don't even keep the key files on the machine, but in a central repository such as LDAP. These hosts run a command to retrieve a user's key file. Rather than using the file argument, use the *authorized_keys_command* argument and the path to the command.

```
auth  sufficient  pam_ssh_agent_auth.so \
  authorized_keys_command=/bin/getkeys.sh
```

The command to fetch a user's key file runs with a single argument, the user whose keys it needs to retrieve. Pam_ssh_agent_auth normally uses the user that's trying to authenticate. If you want to always retrieve a specific user's keys, though, you can add the *authorized_keys_command_user* option and the desired user.

```
auth  sufficient  pam_ssh_agent_auth.so \
  authorized_keys_command=/bin/getkeys.sh \
  authorized_keys_command_user=sysadmins
```

These options should let you put your key files anywhere that fits your environment.

Key File Ownership

Pam_ssh_agent_auth assumes that key files in a user's home directory should be owned by the user. Key files that are not in the user's
home directory should be owned by **root**. It's possible that you might
allow a user to edit their own key file in a central repository like
/etc/ssh/keys, but it's so uncommon that you need to tell pam_ssh_
agent_auth about it with the *allow_user_owned_authorized_keys_file*
option.

Other Options

If you have trouble with pam_ssh_agent_auth, definitely try the
ever-popular debug option. The module will log its progress to the
system's secure authentication log.

Pam_ssh_agent_auth expects to be used with sudo(1). If you compiled sudo to use a non-standard PAM service name, tell the module
about it with the *sudo_service_name* option, an equals sign, and the
service name you chose.

Configuring sudo

The sudo(1) program purges the user's environment before assuming
any privileges. Pam_ssh_agent_auth uses the SSH_AUTH_SOCK
environment variable to find the user's SSH agent. Depending on your
version of sudo and your operating system, you might need to configure sudo(1) to leave the SSH_AUTH_SOCK environment variable in
place. The following sudoers entry accomplishes this.

```
Defaults env_keep += "SSH_AUTH_SOCK"
```

As I write this, CentOS does not require this setting, while Debian
and FreeBSD do.

Pam_ssh_agent_auth and PAM

So, how do you use this thing? Find your system's PAM configuration for sudo(1). In most Linux systems it'll be in */etc/pam.d/sudo*, while FreeBSD will stick it in */usr/local/etc/pam.d/sudo*.

Now the hard part: decide how you want to use the module.

Would you like SSH agent authentication to be sufficient to get sudo access? Put the module at the top of the auth policy and use the sufficient control.

You want to require both an SSH agent and a password? Stick pam_ssh_agent_auth somewhere before the final pam_deny.so and use the required control.

Let's look at a slightly more multi-factor authentication method now.

Chapter 9: One-Time Passwords:
Google Authenticator

A one-time password is a password that works only once. We've had many one-time password implementations, from One-Time Passwords in Everything (OPIE) to RSA tokens. The Time-Based One-Time Passwords system, or TOTP, uses the system clock and a shared secret to compute a valid password on demand. The best known TOTP implementation is Google Authenticator.

Google Authenticator does not require access to Google. The reason it's called *Google Authenticator* is because Google provides the software, not because it hooks into Google's systems in any way. GA works fine on machines not even connected to the Internet.

Google Authenticator transforms your smartphone, tablet, or Chrome browser into an authentication token, using a client-side app and the Google Authenticator PAM module. When you attempt to access a service using Google Authenticator, the PAM module computes a six-digit passcode as a temporary one-time password. The server prompts you for this passcode. Your device computes the current correct passcode for this host, using the same method. Enter the passcode your device offers into the application. If both devices made the same computation, the passcodes match and you get access.

Google Authenticator is a better multi-factor authentication method than using your SSH agent, but it's not perfect. Any tablet, smartphone, or Chrome browser can become an authentication token. If the bad guys capture any of your devices, or steal the shared secret used to configure the client app, they have your authentication token. But at least the devices are physical objects, not a file that intruders can easily copy.[17]

Every host using GA has a separate GA configuration and a unique shared secret. Each user must log on to each host that she's supposed to access and configure her GA access. Google Authenticator, by itself, is best suited to environments with only a few servers and a few accounts. You wouldn't want to have a host with several thousand accounts using plain Google Authenticator unless you dedicate staff time to managing authentication. You can share a GA configuration between hosts, as we'll discuss later, but this alters GA's security profile and requires additional scripting and configuration. We'll start with the simplest case, setting up GA on a single host.

Before even starting with Google Authenticator, check the clocks and time zones on your hosts. Google Authenticator works best on servers with clocks synchronized to the rest of the world. System clocks often skew away from real time, especially on virtual machines. Use ntpd(8) or another time-keeping software to nail your servers' clocks to everyone else's. If GA inexplicably fails, double-check everything's clock and time zone.

Only use Google Authenticator with auth policies. It provides no services to the account, session, or password types.

---

17   Unless you backup the shared secret in a place intruders can steal it from. Don't do that.

Google Authenticator works almost everywhere; it has no environmental requirements like pam_ssh_agent_auth. I encourage you to think carefully before applying it to all system authentication, however. What happens when the server's time gets drunk and skews wildly? If you require GA to log in at the console, fixing the problem will require getting into single user mode, probably via a reboot. Do you have enough redundancy to handle that? Also, Google Authenticator has built-in login rate limiting. If you require GA for both SSH and `sudo`, you'll faceplant straight into that rate limiting.

Carefully consider the implications of your deployment decisions.

Installing Google Authenticator

The Google Authenticator client is easy. Grab your app from the device's app store, or install the Authenticator Chrome extension for your desktop.

Each server that you want to use Google Authenticator must have the Google Authenticator PAM module installed. FreeBSD has a pam_google_authenticator package, but most users will also want to install the libqrencode package. Debian includes the libpam-google-authenticator package, but it's rarely current. No official package for CentOS exists, although as of this writing EPEL includes packages for CentOS 6 and earlier. To use Google Authenticator on a current version of CentOS, or a current Google Authenticator on Debian, you probably must install from source.

Grab the current source code from https://github.com/google/google-authenticator, either with git(1) or by downloading and extracting the zip file. The `libpam` directory contains the Google Authenticator PAM module. Go into that directory to build and install the library.

```
# ./bootstrap.sh
# ./configure
# make
# make install
```

You now have the Google Authenticator PAM module and attendant programs available.

Google Authenticator User Features

Many GA tutorials tell users to run `google-authenticator` and answer `yes` to all its questions. That way lies madness. A user who makes poor decisions can ruin their day and, worse, annoy the helpdesk. Give your users very strict instructions on how to configure the client or, better still, script it for them.

Passcode Types

GA supports two types of passcodes: time-based and counter-based.

The *time-based* method combines the shared secret and the current time to create a temporary one-time password. These passcodes are good for only 30 seconds or so. The time-based one-time passwords are documented in RFC 6238.

Counter-based passcodes compute a series of passcodes, each of which can be used only once. It's a simple list, without any dependency on time. Counter-based passcodes are based on RFC 4226.

Both methods require synchronization between server and device. Time-based passcodes require agreement between the clock on the device and that on the server. Counter-based passcodes require that the user avoid butt-dialing hundreds of passcodes during dinner. While I can conceive circumstances where counter-based passcodes make sense, out here in drafty reality I recommend time-based passcodes.

File Management

Google Authenticator uses the file $HOME/.google_authenticator to manage a user's authentication settings and the current authentication state. (The sysadmin can change the file location, as we'll discuss later.) Even rate limiting takes place in this file.

Timing and Rate Limiting

Intruders trying to gain access to authenticated services use brute force attacks, where they try hundreds or thousands of credentials a minute to see if any of them work. The odds of any one set of credentials working is very low, but computers are incredibly patient and don't mind trying every possible combination until something clicks. Every service needs rate limiting to choke this sort of attack from a torrent to a trickle. If your service has no other way of rate limiting, Google Authenticator can rate limit how many times a passcode can be used and how frequently a user can authenticate.

GA suggests that you allow each passcode to be used only once. For some environments, this makes perfect sense. The Open Authentication (OATH) standard used by many organizations requires one-time-only passcodes.

Some of us have looser security requirements and find one-time-only passcodes intolerable. If solving an urgent problem requires logging into a server and assessing its condition, I don't want one SSH session: I want three or four terminal windows, and I want them *now*. If I use GA to authenticate both SSH and sudo(1), and each passcode can be used only once, gaining privileged access takes even longer.

Even in an environment that doesn't need OATH and has looser security requirements, if you're using GA to allow access to an unencrypted service, allowing each passcode to be used only once makes complete sense. Choose the solution that meets your organization's needs.

Users can adjust clock sensitivity. Each time-based passcode is valid for 30 seconds. The GA PAM module permits a small amount of clock skew by default, treating the previous and next passcodes as valid. With properly synchronized clocks, the user's passcode is good for about 90 seconds. The user can crank this up in her GA configuration file.

Google Authenticator can also restrict the user to no more than three login attempts every 30 seconds. Power users and sysadmins will find this more palatable than permitting only one login. Allowing multiple login attempts violates OATH standards, though.

All of these options are set in the user configuration program.

GA User Configuration

To configure GA, each user needs a device with suitable software and a per-user configuration.

Device Software

The official Google Authenticator software is available for many smartphones, tablets, and the Chrome browser. As the one-time passcodes are based on publicly available standards, though, people have written other applications that can act as GA clients. There's a Firefox plug-in. Authy (https://www.authy.com) is one popular choice. Windows users might prefer WinAuth (https:// winauth.com). Check around and find a client you like.

The easiest way to configure a device requires a QR code reader. The Google Authenticator installer recommends one for your device if you don't have one.

My examples use the official Google Authenticator client. While my test equipment is a Chrome browser and a couple of Android devices, the official GA client should work identically on other platforms and operating systems.

Install your chosen client on your device before proceeding.

User Configuration

Before configuring PAM, log onto the server that's going to use Google Authenticator. Run `google-authenticator` to create a configuration.

```
$ google-authenticator
```

The program asks a series of questions to determine how your account should authenticate.

```
Do you want authentication tokens to be time-based (y/n) y
```

Use time-based codes, as discussed earlier.

The setup program immediately spits out a device configuration, including a secret key, a QR code, and a URL. It also offers five one-time codes. These codes and links are not yet permanent, however. Before making them permanent, use one of them to configure your device.

If your server has the libqrencode library installed, `google-authenticator` displays a QR code. Using the QR code is the easiest way to get the shared secret on your phone. Capture the QR code on your device, and it automatically configures Google Authenticator for the device.

If you're using Chrome as your Google Authenticator device, copy the URL into the browser. You're ready to go.

If neither method works in your setting, `google-authenticator` also displays the shared secret, an annoying long string. Manually enter it into your device.

With any of these three setup methods, your GA app should immediately begin displaying six-digit codes.

Copy the secret and the emergency scratch codes to a safe location, preferably on paper. You might even print the QR code, write the server name on top of the page, and stuff it in a locked drawer. You'll need the emergency and QR codes if you lose your device or things go terribly wrong, as discussed in "Device Theft" and "Disaster Recovery" later this chapter.

Once your device knows about the code, make it permanent by updating the user's GA configuration file.

```
Do you want me to update your
"/home/mwl/.google_authenticator" file (y/n) y
```

Answer n, and the setup program discards all of the codes. Answer y, and your account is ready for GA.

You then get three questions on how the user's GA should behave. We discussed these options in "Google Authenticator User Features" earlier this chapter. Hopefully you decided how GA should behave before getting this far.

```
Do you want to disallow multiple uses of the same au-
thentication token? This restricts you to one login
about every 30s, but it increases your chances to notice
or even prevent man-in-the-middle attacks (y/n) y
```

Answering y means that users can authenticate only once every 30 seconds. Answering n means that codes are reusable while valid.

```
By default, tokens are good for 30 seconds and in order
to compensate forpossible time-skew between the client
and the server, we allow an extra token before and after
the current time. If you experience problems with poor-
time synchronization, you can increase the window from
its default size of 1:30min to about 4min. Do you want
to do so (y/n) y
```

Answering y extends an individual passcode's lifespan. Answering n leaves it at the default.

```
If the computer that you are logging into isn't hard-
ened against brute-forcelogin attempts, you can enable
rate-limiting for the authentication module.By default,
this limits attackers to no more than 3 login attempts
every 30s.Do you want to enable rate-limiting (y/n) y
```

Answering y limits logon attempts to three every 30 seconds. Answering n disables rate limiting.

Scripting User Setup

The Google Authenticator user setup process is simple. Surely your users can handle typing y, capturing a QR code, and typing a specific sequence of three y's and n's?

Anyone who's been a sysadmin more than a week knows the answer to this question is "absolutely not." If more than a couple people will use a service protected by GA, script the configuration process. Here's a simple script that runs `google-authenticator` and answers y twice and n three times.

```
#/bin/sh
printf 'y\ny\nn\nn\nn\n' | google-authenticator
```

The \n is a return, or the ENTER key. The `printf` command spits out y-ENTER, y-ENTER, n-ENTER, n-ENTER, n-ENTER, and feeds them into `google-authenticator`. A user running this script gets their QR code, URL, secret, and their emergency scratch codes without making any decisions at all.

If you run `google-authenticator -h`, you'll get a list of command-line flags and options that let you pre-answer questions. Write your script however you like.

If your organization is large enough, your script should probably hide all output other than the QR code, URL, and secret. You might even strip the output down to the QR code.

GA and PAM

After configuring your account, you can run right to your service's PAM configuration and activate pam_google_authenticator. (If you want to use GA with SSH, remember to review the SSH and PAM information in Chapter 0.)

```
auth required pam_google_authenticator.so
```

But what if you have users other than yourself? Users need to log on to the host to configure GA, but enabling GA locks them out. Bootstrap around this problem with the `nullok` option. Users who lack a GA configuration can log in without one. Once a GA configuration exists, though, the user must enter the code to log in.

```
auth   required   pam_google_authenticator.so nullok
```

If you do this, have the system dump the user straight into the Google Authentication configuration script. Otherwise, some of your users will never actually configure GA. To truly enforce multi-factor authentication with many users on many servers, you must centrally manage GA.

Central GA Management

Enterprises with many servers almost certainly use a management tool such as Ansible or Puppet to hold their environments together. The organization's sysadmins have much better things to do than nursemaid users, copy configuration files around, and restart services. Enterprise software *must* be centrally managed.

The default Google Authenticator configuration assumes that users are trusted. Enterprise authentication systems do not trust users. Enterprise users can, say, change their passwords, but can't be permitted to disable rate limiting. Google Authenticator can be used in these environments.

Each user's *$HOME/.google_authenticator* file doesn't only contain the user's shared secret. It also contains the user's timing, rate limiting, and clock sensitivity settings. Every organization has clever folks who can figure out how to play with the system, and unwise enough to try it. Plus, sometimes the user's home directory is encrypted or mounted via NFS, and thus unavailable until after authentication completes. Using Google Authenticator in these enterprises requires removing the file from the user's control, through the `file` and `owner` options.

The `file` option lets the sysadmin set a different location for the user's *.google_authenticator* file. Use an equals sign and a file location. The option recognizes the variables ~ and `${HOME}` as the user's home directory, and `${USER}` as the username.

```
auth   required   pam_google_authenticator.so \
           file=/u1/ga/${USER}/.google_authenticator
```

Here, each user's GA configuration is located outside her home directory. This lets the system wait to mount the home directory until after authentication completes. By using a user-specific directory owned by the user, each user can continue to manage her own GA configuration. The file should be owned by the user and have mode 400.

You might not want the user to manage their own GA configuration. More than one organization has their users configure their Google Authenticator on a tightly protected enrollment server. The enrollment server automatically propagates that configuration to all other servers in the organization. Users in such enterprises should not have access to edit their config files on all the other servers, and probably not on the enrollment server either. (The enrollment script probably hides everything except the QR code from the user.) In this case the file should be owned by a system user, and the user forbidden to access the file itself. Use the `user` option for this.

```
auth  required  pam_google_authenticator.so \
  secret=/etc/ga/${USER} user=google
```

Here, the user's GA configuration is stashed in the directory /etc/ga, in a file named after the user. My authentication config would be /etc/ga/mwl. The file is owned by the user **google**, and should have mode 400. While sysadmins can easily identify an individual user's file, the only way the configuration gets updated is through the management system.

Not allowing the user access to their configuration prevents Google Authenticator from using certain functions. The module keeps all time-keeping information in the configuration file. If the user cannot update the file, the rate limiting functions will not work. During setup, answer n to all functions except writing the original file.

While using Google Authenticator in this manner requires additional programming, it's no worse than using other "enterprise-ready" token systems.

Time Skew Adjustment

Google Authenticator can try to account for an inaccurate system clock. Unsuccessfully authenticating three times, each 30 seconds apart, suggests to the GA PAM module that the clock is skewed and hints at how bad the skew is.

Use the *noskewadj* option to turn off this behavior. If the system clock is so inaccurate that skew adjustments make sense, fixing the clock makes more sense than subtly insinuating there's a problem.

Passcode Display

Much like passwords, passcodes are not echoed back to the user. To echo the passcode back to the user, use the module option *echo_verification_code*.

Passcodes are ephemeral entities. In many deployments, a passcode can be used only once. Even if someone peers over the user's shoulder to capture the passcode, it expires in a minute or so. Most of the time, displaying the entered passcode for the user vastly reduces support calls. Users—yes, even *your* users—can recognize they typed the wrong six numbers when they're visible.

Simultaneous Passcode and Password Entry

Some PAM-enabled applications and modules (such as Radius authentication or SSH with `PasswordAuthentication` set to `yes`) don't cope well with multiple authentication prompts. You can tell Google Authenticator to ask for both the password and the passcode in a single request by using the *forward_pass* option. GA will digest the passcode, but hand the password on to the next module. The next module must use the *use_first_pass* option to accept the forwarded password.

```
auth  required  pam_google_authenticator.so forward_pass
auth  sufficient  pam_unix.so try_first_pass
```

A user attempting to authenticate will get a single prompt, like so.

```
Password & verification code:
```

The user needs to enter her password, a space, and the Google Authenticator passcode. If the passcode is correct, GA forwards the password to the next module. In this case, as the next module is sufficient, a correct password immediately permits access.

You cannot combine forward_pass and echo_verification_code. Well, you *can*, but the GA PAM module will both echo the password with the passcode and reject the authentication request, so the combination is not useful.

119

New Devices

Once Google Authenticator is configured, you can pretty much ignore it… until you get a new smartphone, tablet, or computer. You'll probably want to configure your new device with the same authentication settings as the old one. Sometimes, you literally exchange your old phone for a new one.

Remember when I said to back up the security code when you first configure your account for GA? This is exactly why. Google Authenticator won't re-display the secret, the configuration URL, or the QR code from an existing installation. You must use the backup copy you kept. Manually entering the security code is annoying, but far better than reconfiguring all of your servers and loading those new configurations on all of your other devices.

Disaster Recovery

With Google Authenticator you might have two separate kinds of disaster: a stolen device, or a broken PAM module. Both have similar disaster recovery considerations.

Losing one of the factors of your multi-factor authentication system is not disastrous, but it does require quick, deliberate action. If you lose both the device *and* the password, SSH keys, or other authentication, act with a speed just short of panic. Have the affected user re-run the `google-authenticator` or your organization's wrapper script on all affected hosts. If the situation is urgent, use su(1) to run it for the user.

Another disaster would be when a system's clock breaks. The GA passcode won't work then.

When you run `google-authenticator`, it presents five eight-digit codes after the QR code. These are *emergency codes*. The user can use them to authenticate, but each code works only once. If you backed up these codes and have them available, you can use them to get into the system and fix the time. If you run low on emergency codes, re-run `google-authenticator` to change your secret and generate new emergency codes.[18]

GA removes the one-time code from the user's configuration before permitting access. This requires that the user have write access to her configuration file. If your user configurations are owned by a different user, the emergency codes will not work.

GA File Format

Google Authenticator's configuration file, `.google_authenticator`, includes only a few possible options.

```
5KPJYOJZCY67OENW
" RATE_LIMIT 3 30
" WINDOW_SIZE 17
" DISALLOW_REUSE
" TOTP_AUTH
21481565
...
```

The first line is always the shared secret. Don't muck with it. Not all possible codes are valid, so you can't set a corporate standard that each user's secret is their first name and their Social Security number.

The presence of the RATE_LIMIT option enables rate limiting. It takes two arguments: how many authentication attempts to allow, and how many seconds they're allowed in. Rate limiting requires that the user be able to write to the configuration file.

---

18   Or you could, you know, fix your servers' clocks once and for all. But if you haven't done that by now, I certainly can't convince you.

The WINDOW_SIZE option dictates how time-sensitive your passcode is. A `1` means that only the precisely current passcode, as dictated by the system clock, will be acceptable. Each increase of two means that an extra passcode before and after the current one is acceptable. Setting this to `17`, the value used if you take the `google-authenticator` suggestion of allowing a four-minute window, means that the passcode for the current time, plus eight earlier codes and eight later ones, is acceptable.

The DISALLOW_REUSE option means that each passcode can be used once and only once.

The file ends with the user's remaining one-time passcodes. While it might be tempting to add your own one-time codes to this file, GA performs additional verification on the emergency codes. Adding `00000001` to the end of the file won't work. Plus, the act of editing an emergency code invalidates the remaining emergency codes.

Now that we've secured remote access, let's consider something useful to local users.

Chapter 10: Console Access with SSH Keys

Sysadmins have a morning routine. After caffeine, pants, more caffeine, and staggering into the office, we slump in front of our workstation. We log on with a username and password. The majority enter our SSH passphrase and load our keys into an SSH agent. At that point we can start work. This requires authenticating to our workstation twice: once with a username and password, and once with a username and SSH key.

The *pam_ssh* module integrates SSH key management with the login process. A user can go to their workstation and log in with only their SSH key. Rather than authenticating against `/etc/passwd`, the user authenticates with the SSH private key in their account. On successful authentication, pam_ssh starts an SSH agent and stores the decrypted private key in the agent.

Unlike other PAM modules discussed in this book, pam_ssh is most useful for workstations, and then only select ones. You certainly wouldn't want to authenticate to a server based on SSH key files stored on that server. Typical users should *never* offer passphrases to a remote server. You probably wouldn't want to have this functionality on the salesperson's machine. But many sysadmins find pam_ssh quite convenient on their personal laptops.

Pam_ssh provides service to the auth and session types. Used in an auth policy, pam_ssh prompts the user for a passphrase. It attempts to decrypt the user's private SSH keys with that passphrase, much as ssh(1) or ssh-add(1) do. If the passphrase works, the module returns PAM_SUCCESS. Otherwise, the module fails. In a session policy, pam_ssh starts an SSH agent for the user and adds the key to the agent.

FreeBSD includes pam_ssh by default. Centos has a pam_ssh package, while Debian offers a libpam-ssh package. These modules are not only packaged differently; they're different code. FreeBSD imported the original pam_ssh and made improvements. That code was extracted from FreeBSD and forked into slightly different versions for CentOS and Debian. Each supports different features. We'll cover each operating system's pam_ssh separately.

Additionally, each operating system uses pam_ssh differently. We'll use this module as an opportunity to explore how a very similar module can be configured with entirely different PAM statements and produce very different behavior.

All of the versions of pam_ssh we cover support the try_first_pass, use_first_pass, and debug options.

One Module, Different Policies

All three of our target platforms deploy pam_ssh differently. CentOS does not offer any suggestions on placing pam_ssh statements. FreeBSD includes pam_ssh in the default install. Statements for pam_ssh appear in FreeBSD's standard configuration files, but they're commented out. Debian's libpam-ssh package not only installs pam_ssh, but also adds PAM statements to enable the module.

We'll consider the simpler FreeBSD case first, then Debian.

FreeBSD and pam_ssh

FreeBSD offers examples of enabling pam_ssh systemwide and in individual services. I don't want to use pam_ssh to authenticate to the FTP server on my workstation, or over a serial line, so I won't enable it systemwide. I *do* want to use it during a graphical console logon, however. The file `/etc/pam.d/xdm` has commented-out entries for pam_ssh. Uncommenting them gives us these auth and session policies.

```
auth     sufficient  pam_ssh.so       no_warn try_first_pass
auth     required    pam_unix.so      no_warn try_first_pass
session  required    pam_ssh.so       want_agent
session  required    pam_lastlog.so   no_fail
```

The auth policy has only two statements. The first, pam_ssh, is sufficient. The logon will prompt the user for their SSH key's passphrase. If the passphrase is correct, the sufficient statement means that access is immediately granted. The no_warn flag disables warnings. and The try_first_pass flag tells pam_ssh to try any earlier password. As this is the first statement in the policy, there won't be an earlier password.

The second auth statement, for pam_unix, is for traditional Unix authentication against `/etc/passwd`. This auth rule gets triggered only if pam_ssh fails. With the try_first_pass argument, this module attempts to use the previously entered SSH key passphrase as a Unix system password. If you accidentally enter your password instead of your passphrase, the system lets you in.

Taken together, these mean that the user is first prompted for a username and an SSH passphrase. If he doesn't enter the correct passphrase, he's prompted for a username and password.

In the session policy, the pam_ssh module sets up the user's SSH agent. The want_agent option is FreeBSD-specific, and is discussed in the FreeBSD section. The session policy also performs logging with pam_lastlog.

Other X managers, such as Gnome's `gdm`, will need similar PAM rule entries in their `/usr/local/etc/pam.d` files.

For a completely different take on deploying pam_ssh, consider Debian.

Debian and pam_ssh

When you install libpam-ssh on Debian, the package automatically adds pam_ssh rules to `/etc/pam.d/common-auth` and `/etc/pam.d/common-session`. This enables SSH key authentication for every service that uses the common rules. If that host runs Telnet or FTP servers, they'll authenticate against the user's SSH key and transmit the user's passphrase across the network in clear text.[19]

Here's Debian's `/etc/pam.d/common-auth`, with the comments removed. While Debian admins should read those comments, we can study the PAM policy without them.

```
auth    [success=1 default=ignore]  pam_unix.so    nullok_secure
auth    requisite                   pam_deny.so
auth    required                    pam_permit.so
auth    optional                    pam_ssh.so     use_first_pass
```

The first statement calls pam_unix to perform traditional authentication against the password file. It uses extended Linux controls rather than standard PAM controls. If the user enters a correct username and password, PAM skips one statement in the policy. On any other response, the pam_unix module is ignored and we fall through to the second statement.

_____

19   Just to be clear: this is bad. Of course, if you're providing telnet services, you're pretty much doomed anyway.

The second statement calls pam_deny, which summarily rejects any authentication attempt. It's a requisite rule, so the rejection takes place immediately. At first glance, this looks ridiculous—why automatically reject absolutely everything right near the beginning of the policy? The only way to reach the statement is by failing to pass pam_unix's password authentication, however. If the hapless user successfully authenticated in the first statement, the authentication policy skips this step.

The third statement uses pam_permit. If the user successfully authenticates with a username and password in rule one, they get dumped here. It's a required rule, but a call to pam_permit always succeeds. The first three statements, taken as a whole, mean "the user must authenticate with a username and password, or their login is rejected."

The fourth statement calls the pam_ssh module. It's optional—the user does not have to enter a correct SSH passphrase to log on. A username and password are sufficient. The standard Debian pam_ssh statement shown uses the use_first_pass option, though. This tells PAM to recycle the password the user entered earlier, and feed it to pam_ssh. If the password doesn't work with pam_ssh, don't prompt again.

The upshot is, Debian's standard configuration assumes that your SSH passphrase is the same as your password. Long-time SSH users experimenting with pam_ssh on Debian will find this surprising. Passphrases should be much longer than passwords: that's why they're *phrases* and not *words*.

If you're using pam_ssh on Debian, and don't want to use a single word as your SSH passphrase, you can either remove the use_first_pass option from the pam_ssh auth statement or change your password to be your passphrase. Debian lets you have very long passwords.

Now let's take a quick look at the session rules.

```
session [default=1]   pam_permit.so
session requisite     pam_deny.so
session required      pam_permit.so
session required      pam_unix.so
session optional      pam_ssh.so
session optional      pam_tmpdir.so
```

The first three statements are similar to the first statements in the auth policy. There's a requisite pam_deny, but you literally can never hit it. The real rules begin with the fourth statement, which calls pam_unix to set up the user's environment. Rule five, for pam_ssh, enables the user's SSH agent. The final statement calls pam_tmpdir to configure a secure temporary directory for the user.

Comparison

Why do FreeBSD and Debian have such wildly different policies for a similar function? Part of this is because Debian's policies are designed to be friendly for the pam-auth-update(8) PAM configuration tool. FreeBSD assumes you'll be editing your own PAM rules, and hence you understand what each type of statement does.

Another key difference, though, is that the operating system packagers make different assumptions about how the module will be used. FreeBSD's developers assume that authentication via the user's SSH key is sufficient, and entirely skip authenticating against the system password file. Debian, on the other hand, requires the user to authenticate against the password file—but it assumes the user's passphrase is the same as their password.

The real problem here is the word "assumes."

If you hear about a cool PAM module and try to deploy it, you must carefully check your assumptions, the assumptions of the module authors, and the assumptions made by the folks packaging the module for your operating system. If you're using third-party documentation, check the author's assumptions as well. The only way to truly understand how a module works is to carefully read the PAM policy, statement by statement. I had deployed FreeBSD's pam_ssh several times, but the first time I tried pam_ssh on Debian it drove me to the edge of madness[20] until I carefully unraveled the PAM configuration.

Assumptions with PAM will ruin your day, your week, your everything until you carefully dissect your configuration.

Speaking of assumptions: you also can't assume that modules named X are the same between platforms, even if they have similar functions. The pam_ssh module differs between FreeBSD, CentOS, and Debian, as we'll see shortly.

SSH and pam_ssh

A proper SSH key has a passphrase several words long or longer. During normal use, you type a passphrase only rarely. When you're first experimenting with pam_ssh, however, you can expect to type the passphrase repeatedly. I recommend creating a testing-only SSH key with a simple, easily typed passphrase for use while figuring out your pam_ssh configuration. Don't install the test key on any servers. Once you have pam_ssh working as desired, erase the test key.

The next question you might have is, did my login successfully decrypt my key and add it to my agent? On systems like Debian that assume your password is your passphrase, that's an important detail. Check the keys in your agent with `ssh-add -l`.

---

20   Okay, fine. "…drove me to this quaint little town called Screaming Rage, about ten miles into Madness, and shoved me out of the car without slowing down." Happy now?

```
$ ssh-add -l
2048 8c:f9:2d:…:91 testlab 2016-02-01 RSA
```

From here, manage your SSH session and keys normally.

When using SSH passphrases for authentication, a key without a passphrase is like an account without a password. Pam_ssh normally ignores keys without passphrases: it won't use them for authentication and it won't add them to the SSH agent.

If you want to permit authentication using a key without a passphrase, use the *nullok* option in the pam_ssh auth statement. All three pam_ssh versions support nullok. Permitting authentication using passphrase-free keys is a terrible idea. It's even worse than allowing an account without a password, because that passphrase-free key might grant access to other hosts.

All of these pam_ssh implementations allow logons with the private key file *$HOME/.ssh/identity*. This key file is used for version 1 of the SSH protocol. This version isn't merely obsolete—it is actively broken. Anyone who can capture your traffic can decrypt it. We aren't quite at the stage of "if you're running SSHv1, turn it off and enable Telnet; it might be insecure, but it doesn't pretend to be secure," but that day is coming quickly. If you have an old SSHv1 key lying around, verify that none of your SSH servers support SSHv1, double-check that your modern SSH keys are installed everywhere, and relegate your *identity* key to backup.

No pam_ssh implementation supports the AuthorizedKeysCommand used by sshd(8). The AuthorizedKeysCommand option provides only public keys, not the private keys used for authentication. Your private keys belong on a workstation, not on the network.

FreeBSD pam_ssh

FreeBSD ships with pam_ssh installed, and many FreeBSD PAM configurations in `/etc/pam.d` have commented-out auth and session pam_ssh entries. Some of these strike me as rather odd (using pam_ssh to authenticate FTP, thus transmitting your passphrase in clear text?), but none of them are mandatory. Activating those rules for login attempts in `/etc/pam.d/login` or `/etc/pam.d/system` changes the user's login prompt.

```
login: mwl
SSH passphrase:
```

Enter your SSH passphrase. The pam_ssh module will try to decrypt every standard key file in your `.ssh` directory: `id_ecdsa`, `id_dsa`, `id_rsa`, and `identity`. If you type the passphrase correctly, the sufficient control says "Login is permitted, end the policy now!" and you get access.

Pam_ssh supports the common debug, use_first_pass, and try_first_pass options discussed in Chapter 1.

OpenPAM SSH Agent

When pam_ssh decrypts a user's keys, the session pam_ssh statement starts an SSH agent and adds the decrypted key to the agent. But if pam_ssh cannot decrypt any keys, it doesn't start an agent. Instead, PAM proceeds directly to the next statement in the session policy. The end result is that if a user logs on with an SSH passphrase, he gets an SSH agent. If he logs on with a password, he gets no SSH agent.

The sysadmin might want users who log on with a password to unilaterally get an SSH agent, though. Adding the *want_agent* option to the pam_ssh session statement triggers starting an SSH agent at logon, even without loading any keys into it. The want_agent option appears in the commented-out FreeBSD statements.

Key Selection

FreeBSD's pam_ssh automatically tries to decrypt the key files *identity*, *id_rsa*, *id_dsa*, and *id_ecdsa* in the user's *$HOME/.ssh* directory. Keys with different names are not decrypted by the login process.

You cannot remove any of these keys from pam_ssh's check. For that you'd need to use a different version of pam_ssh, such as that found in CentOS.

CentOS pam_ssh

CentOS' EPEL repository includes a pam_ssh package. Unlike FreeBSD and Debian, CentOS doesn't include any PAM policy statements with the package. You must decide how to use pam_ssh, and create rules for your auth and session policies.

Here, I've added pam_ssh to */etc/pam.d/login*, the PAM configuration for plain text console logins for CentOS 7.2. We'll start with the auth policy.

```
auth [user_unknown=ignore success=ok ignore=ignore \
     default=bad] pam_securetty.so
auth     [success=1 default=ignore]  pam_ssh.so
auth     substack  system-auth
auth     include   postlogin
```

The first statement in the auth policy is the usual pam_securetty rule checking for a secure terminal.

The second statement inserts pam_ssh into the policy. Rather than using a standard control, however, I use Linux-PAM extended controls. If pam_ssh returns anything other than PAM_SUCCESS, we ignore pam_ssh and the policy proceeds normally. If a user successfully enters her passphrase and pam_ssh can decrypt the user's private key, PAM skips the next rule.

The next rule is the substack for normal system authentication. Giving pam_ssh a working passphrase lets the policy skip the entire normal Unix-style authentication process.

The last rule includes the normal post-login processing. No matter if the user logged on with a passphrase or a password, CentOS performs its logging and accounting.

The session rules are simpler. Put your pam_ssh statement right before including the system-auth file, so that your SSH agent starts before the rest of your environment gets set up. It really could go anywhere in the session policy *after* the `pam_selinux.so open` rule.

```
...
session    optional    pam_ssh.so
session    include     system-auth
...
```

At a PAM level, you're ready.

On modern CentOS, though, you're almost certainly using SELinux. If you have trouble with your SSH agent, check `/var/log/secure`. Permissions errors on starting your agent are almost certainly related to SELinux. Chapter 6 discusses fixing SELinux-related PAM issues, using pam_ssh as an example.

CentOS pam_ssh Login Prompt

Unlike OpenPAM, CentOS' pam_ssh doesn't present the user with a "passphrase" prompt. Users see the same `Password:` prompt that always appears. CentOS makes pam_ssh all stealthy. The user needs to know that entering their SSH passphrase is an option.

With the statements given earlier this section, a user who doesn't enter a passphrase has their authentication attempt fall through to the system-auth substack, where pam_unix's try_first_pass option means it will try to use whatever the user entered as a password.

133

Choosing Key Files

Specify which SSH private key files pam_ssh attempts to decrypt with the *keyfiles* option. CentOS defaults to checking the `id_dsa`, `id_rsa`, and `identity` files. The `identity` file is used for only the long-broken SSH version 1 protocol, and I would encourage you to disable it in pam_ssh.

```
auth  [success=1 default=ignore]  pam_ssh.so \
      keyfiles=id_dsa,id_rsa
```

You can add non-standard keys files here as desired.

If you want sophisticated key selection, check out Debian's pam_ssh.

Debian pam_ssh

Debian offers pam_ssh in the libpam-ssh package. We discussed Debian's pam_ssh policy in length earlier this chapter, so let's plunge straight into how the module works. Remember that Debian's default pam_ssh configuration expects your SSH passphrase to be the same as your password, though.

The interesting thing about Debian's pam_ssh is that it offers users great control over which keys can be used for authentication and which keys get added to the SSH agent.

Debian pam_ssh Key Selection

Debian's pam_ssh ignores all the usual key files, and instead relies on the directories `$HOME/.ssh/login-keys.d` and `$HOME/.ssh/session-keys.d`. These directories don't exist by default; the user must create them.

The `login-keys.d` directory contains SSH private key files that can be used for authentication. Files here can be the actual private keys, or symlinks to the key files. Here I go into my login keys directory and link to my standard SSH key.

```
$ cd .ssh/login-keys.d
$ ln -s ../id_rsa
```

When I log onto the system, pam_ssh checks this directory. It attempts to use the user-provided password to decrypt any private keys it finds. It adds any keys it can decrypt to the user's SSH agent.

The `session-keys.d` directory also contains key files or symlinks to keys. Unlike files in login-keys.d, though, pam_ssh will not use these key files for authentication. Once the user authenticates, however, pam_ssh attempts to use the password to decrypt the keys in the session directory. It adds decrypted keys to the agent.

Bypassing Passwords

Maybe you don't want a long password, instead relying on the passphrase alone for console access. This would let you separate authentication methods for clear-text protocols like FTP from logons via SSH or the console. You can accomplish this by rearranging Debian's auth policy.

```
auth    sufficient                      pam_ssh.so
auth    [success=1 default=ignore]      pam_unix.so nullok_secure
auth    requisite                       pam_deny.so
auth    required                        pam_permit.so
```

Here I've moved the pam_ssh rule to the top of the auth policy, even before pam_unix. I could use a Linux-PAM extended control much like the pam_unix statement does, but sufficient expresses my desired behavior.

Actually, as I'm manually editing this file and thus making it ineligible for automated management, I'm more likely to redo the entire policy and remove statements that can never be hit.

```
auth   sufficient   pam_ssh.so
auth   required     pam_unix.so nullok_secure
```

If the user cannot authenticate with an SSH key, they must authenticate with a password. I find this much easier to comprehend. On my personal workstation, I might even make pam_ssh required and completely ditch the pam_unix rule.

Other people aren't as security-conscious as I am, though. Their machines need something to make sure they have a decent password, as we'll see in the next chapter.

Chapter 11: Password Quality Checks

The word *password* is a terrible password. Everybody knows that, except users. Several PAM modules let you impose quality standards on your passwords to prevent users from using such obviously bad passwords. These quality checkers won't eliminate bad passwords, but will require users to be much more creative in creating bad passwords.

While everyone agrees that *password* makes a ghastly password, the qualities that make a password good are a subject of contentious debate. Even otherwise calm and rational sysadmins discussing password quality measures with other calm and rational sysadmins have been known to have their quiet and sensible discussion escalate into a knife fight. Some entirely object to the concept of password quality checking as it's used today. For this reason, we won't discuss what characteristics make a password good. Instead, we'll cover PAM modules that allow you to inflict your particular prejudices on your users.

The most common password quality checking module is pam_passwdqc. CentOS 7 eliminated pam_passwdqc, replacing it with pam_pwquality. Debian has packages for both. We'll use pam_passwdqc to explain the configuration and concepts of password quality checking, then briefly touch on pam_pwquality.

Configuring Password Checks

Test a password's quality when the user changes the password. This makes the quality check one of the very few functions that belongs in a password policy, like so.

```
password    requisite   pam_passwdqc.so
password    required    pam_unix.so
```

On most systems, passwd(1) has its own PAM configuration, */etc/pam.d/passwd*. Changes in the system default file won't affect passwd(1), unless */etc/pam.d/passwd* explicitly includes the default.

When pam_unix is satisfied that the password should change, it alters */etc/passwd* and related files. Place any password quality check before the pam_unix statement, so the password is audited before being changed.

Password Rotation

The question "how often should users change passwords?" is intimately tied to password quality checkers. Many organizations require changing passwords at regular intervals. Others argue that requiring password changes is more insecure than leaving them unchanged. Perhaps the password should only be changed upon first login.

You don't set password expiration policies within PAM, but a correctly configured PAM needs to respect password expiration. I've seen more than one LDAP-based network that doesn't reject expired passwords.

BSD systems manage password lifespan globally in */etc/login.conf* and for individual users with pw(8). Linux systems mostly use chage(8). Consult your operating system manual for details on configuring password lifespans.

Quality Concepts

All password quality checkers share certain common concepts.

Character Classes

No, not "fighter," "cleric," "thief," and so on. Password checkers break possible characters in a password into four different classes: lower-case letters, upper-case letters, numbers, and every other ASCII symbol. A fifth character class exists for non-ASCII characters, but most of us can't easily type those. You can require a user's passwords to contain up to four classes, and adjust length requirements based on how many classes a proposed password contains.

Many users build their passwords using a common word as a base. If the sales guy must change his password every month, he might just increment a number at the end, replacing *hamster1* with *hamster2*. Password checkers check for substrings in common between the old and new passwords. You can assign the size of a substring. These checks don't record old passwords—remember, a user must provide their old password before they can enter a new one, so the checker has access to both. These substring checks won't work if **root** barges in and changes the user's password.

Maximum Password Length

In past decades, Unix-like systems had a maximum password length of eight characters. This seems absurd today, but was necessary for the traditional DES password hashes. Even today, add-on system services might have maximum limits on password length. And if you share password files between systems, one of those systems might still use traditional hashes. You need to set a maximum length on system passwords. You also must read the password checker manual page *very* carefully.

If you're running software that has a maximum password length, get the software fixed or replace it. Systems using traditional password hashes are probably decades obsolete, mission-critical, minimally funded, and so poorly understood that nobody dares touch them. Large enterprises and governments are the worst offenders here. Attempting to replace the system will either end your career or, if you're successful, crown you Dark Lord of the IT Department.[21]

pam_passwdqc

The pam_passwdqc module appears almost everywhere except in recent versions of CentOS, and has long been the standard tool for checking the quality of new passwords during password changes. The pam_passwdqc module lets you define password length requirements, the number of characters that must differ between old and new passwords, the type of characters that must be included in a password, and more.

Enabling and Configuring

Both Debian and FreeBSD use pam_passwdqc. The only real difference between them is that FreeBSD requires any options to be placed in the PAM configuration file, while Debian lets you put pam_passwdqc options in a separate file, *passwdqc.conf* with the *config* option.

```
password  requisite  pam_passwdqc config=/etc/passwdqc.conf
```

The actual configuration options that appear in each are identical, however. We'll show examples from both.

Once you enable pam_passwdqc, any time anyone tries to change any password they'll have to pass quality checks first. You can relax this strictness with the *enforce* option.

---

21   You might be a nice person when you start, but the actions needed to replace such a system will transform you into a Dark Lord. That's just how business works.

If you set `enforce=users`, the password checks apply only to unprivileged users. The **root** user can assign a user an inadequate password. They'll get a warning, but the password will get changed.

If you set `enforce=none`, pam_passwdqc prints password requirements, warnings, and hints but doesn't enforce them.

Here I tell pam_passwdqc to allow **root** to violate password standards.

```
password  requisite  pam_passwdqc.so  enforce=users
```

If I've defined a Debian configuration file, this entry can appear on a line by itself.

```
enforce=users
```

Now, when the boss calls complaining that *GolfMaster* is not an acceptable password, I can become **root** and set it for her.

I discourage you from using `enforce=none`, except perhaps during a warning period as you're implementing new password standards. Voluntary standards are ignored standards.

pam_passwdqc Complexity and Length

Pam_passwdqc uses character classes to dictate the minimum acceptable length of a password. The fewer character classes a password has, the longer the password must be. By default, a password that contains only two classes of characters must be 24 characters long. A password that includes three classes of characters must be eight characters long, while including all four character classes reduces the minimum length to seven characters.

The complexity checks have two exceptions. A capital letter at the beginning of the password doesn't count as an additional character class. Neither does a number at the end. The password *Hamster1* counts as one character class, whereas *1hamsteR* contains three. You can explain this to your users, or just tell them that capitals and numbers need to be in the middle of the password to count. They'll curse your name either way.

Set the minimum length of a password of each type with the *min* option. This option requires five numerical, comma-separated arguments. Any of these arguments can also be set to `disabled` to automatically reject passwords of that type.

The first argument dictates the minimum length of passwords with only one character class. This defaults to `disabled`, making pam_passwdqc reject any password made of only one character class.

The second argument gives the minimum length of passwords with two character classes that aren't passphrases. It defaults to 24.

The third argument gives the minimum length, in characters, of passphrases. We discuss passphrases in the next section. Passphrases default to a minimum length of 11 characters.

The fourth argument sets the minimum length of passwords with three character classes. This defaults to eight.

Lastly, the fifth argument gives the minimum length of passwords with four character classes. The default is seven.

This is a weird order; why use it? The arguments are ordered by length. A password with only two character classes needs to be really long to be secure. A passphrase can be a little shorter than that. Passwords with three or four character classes can be shorter still. These numbers must decrease, or pam_passwdqc will die with an error.

You can also set a maximum length with the *max* option, which defaults to 40, but passwords that are too long aren't generally an issue.

Here we disable passwords with only one or two character classes. Passphrases have a minimum length of 16 characters. Passwords with three character classes have a minimum length of 10, while passwords with four character classes have a minimum length of nine.

```
password  requisite  pam_passwdqc.so \
          min=disabled,disabled,16,10,9 max=80
```

I've defined a password's maximum length as 80, just to annoy that one guy from Sales who's read too many Neal Stephenson books and thus thinks he understands security.

Passphrases

Instead of a single password, you might set your password to a phrase like *Lucas needs gelato!* This is a *passphrase*, a series of words instead of a single word. Surprisingly, longer passphrases might actually be more secure than shorter passwords containing random characters. For one thing, your users won't write them down as often. You can test passphrases with pam_passwdqc.

Another advantage to passphrases, from the user's perspective, is that they don't need to have multiple character classes. A passphrase like *correct horse battery staple* contains only one character class but passes the quality check.

The *passphrase* option gives the minimum number of separate words that must be included for the password to be treated as a passphrase. It defaults to three. If a passphrase doesn't have enough words for pam_passwdqc to treat it as a passphrase, it's merely a password that includes spaces and is quality-checked as such.

Here I've used Debian's `passwdqc.conf` to require that passphrases be four or more words.

```
passphrase=4
```

Requiring more words in a passphrase will probably, but not certainly, drive users to create longer passphrases.

Password Similarity

The pam_passwdqc module helps discourage users from using similar passwords with the *match* and *similar* options.

When a user changes his password, pam_passwdqc checks for common substrings within the password. It can recognize these common strings backwards and forwards, such as *hamster1* versus *1retsmah*, and in different cases. The *match* option gives the number of characters that it looks for in such a matching string. The default, four, looks for common strings of four or more characters between the old and new passwords.

```
match=4
```

While these checks are needed to keep users from using predictable password schemes, they can produce unexpected results. Consider changing the password *!meowing6* to *homeowner!AtLast*. The user might be thrilled to have finally bought a home and have adequate space for his half-dozen cats, and at first glance these are both adequate passwords—but both contain the string *meow*.

To turn off these checks, set the option *similar* to `permit`. It defaults to `deny`.

```
similar=permit
```

Disabling the similarity check is either a bad idea, or a terrible idea.

While pam_passwdqc has additional options, they mostly manage edge cases when you want to tweak how the policy as a whole operates.

pam_pwquality

The pam_pwquality module takes a more complex approach to password quality. In addition to setting the requirements for password length and different character classes, it has a "credits" system that allows a shorter password if that password follows good practices. Theoretically, pam_pwquality can identify poor password choices.[22] (This might sound familiar to older sysadmins, as pam_pwquality takes many concepts from the venerable module pam_cracklib.)

Common pam_pwquality Configuration & Behavior

The common options use_first_pass, try_first_pass, and debug work with pam_pwquality. Make copious use of the debug option when you're first experimenting with this module.

You'll often see the *local_users_only* option, telling the module to only check passwords for users with accounts in the local machine's password file.

Use the *retry* option to set how many times pam_pwquality will let the user try to create an acceptable password. Once the user has tried and failed this many times, pam_pwquality throws them out.

Finally, while the *authtok_type* option looks impressive, it only sets a user-visible string to say what kind of password is getting changed. It's normally blank.

The usual pam_pwquality statement looks like this.

```
password  requisite  pam_pwquality.so try_first_pass \
          local_users_only retry=3 authtok_type=
```

The pam_pwquality module rejects entire categories of password out-of-hand. If the new password is the same as the old, with only a change of case, it's rejected. If it's too small, or too much like the old one, it's rejected. If it's a rotated version of the old password, such as *hamster1* and *amster1h*, it's rejected. Finally, palindromes are utterly unacceptable.

---

22   Never underestimate a user's ability to creatively make poor choices

You can fine-tune some of these behaviors. We'll start by establishing minimum requirements, move on to the credits system, and then cover options that apply to both. Other configuration options can go either in a PAM statement, or in `/etc/security/pwquality.conf`.

Setting Password Requirements

You can set restrictions on the user's password by setting a minimum length, the number of character classes needed, and the minimum number of each class of characters.

The *minlen* option sets the minimum length of the password. Increasing the minimum length is easy, but pam_pwquality has hard-coded lower limits. The minimum effective password length on any system is probably six, but this might be reduced to four by re-compiling. The default is eight.

The *minclass* option sets a minimum number of character classes that must be in the password.

Set the minimum number of digits in a password with the *dcredit* option. The *ucredit* option specifies the minimum number of upper-case letters, while *lcredit* sets the minimum number of lower case letters. Finally, *ocredit* sets a minimum number of other characters. Specify minimums as negative numbers—positive values mean you're using the credits system. Here I'm putting specific requirements on user passwords. For clarity, I've omitted the usual `retry` statements and such. You'd certainly want to include them in production.

```
password   requisite  pam_pwquality.so minlen=8 min\
      class=3 dcredit=-2 ucredit=-2 lcredit=-2 ocredit=-2
```

This statement requires the user to have at least two digits, two lower-case letters, two upper-case letters, and two other characters. The minimum length is eight. While I've defined the minimum number of classes as three, that setting isn't exactly used—the minimums in each of the four classes outweigh the minclass statement.

Defined minimum requirements for passwords simplify attacks on your system. If an intruder is trying to guess the passwords for your system, he can skip all of the possible passwords that don't meet your password standards. To make life harder for attackers[23], use the credits system.

Password Quality Credits

The pam_pwquality credits system lets you set a minimum password length, but then gives the user extra credit for including multiple different character classes. This gives flexibility in passwords, but permits people to use shorter passwords if they have a greater variety of characters.

Sysadmins have enough trouble explaining conventional password policies to their users. I have never successfully explained credits to users. In the real world, I find that credits are a bonus for the sysadmin team, not regular users.

With the credits system, the user gets credit for each additional character class that they include in their password. By default, each character class gives one extra credit character. Consider the world's worst password, *password*. It's eight characters long. The user gets one extra credit for including lower case characters, so it's scored as having nine characters. If you set the minimum password length to nine characters, *password* qualifies. (It gets rejected for other reasons, mind you, but on length alone it works.)

Adding a capital letter lets the password be one character shorter, such as *pAsswor*. Stick a number in there, and you can trim the password down to six: *pAssw0*. Six characters, plus one credit each for

---

23   and users

including lower-case, upper-case, and digit characters. Remember, without recompiling, pam_pwquality won't accept passwords less than six characters.

With the credits system, a user who doesn't want to mix characters doesn't have to. A plain eight-character, lower-case password suffices.

When using credits, the options *dcredit*, *ucredit*, *lcredit*, and *ocredit* still apply to digits, uppercase, lowercase, and other characters, respectively. Rather than defining minimum numbers of characters of those classes needed for a password, however, with credits they define the maximum number of credits a user can get for including characters of that type. Setting `ocredit` to 3 means that a user can get up to three credits for having non-alphanumeric characters in her password. Each defaults to `1`.

Consider these `/etc/security/pwquality.conf` settings.

```
minlen=16
ocredit=3
lcredit=0
```

The minimum password length is 16 characters. The user gets no extra credit for using lower case characters, but can have up to three credits from non-alphanumeric characters. There are no special settings for uppercase characters or digits, so they give a credit of one each.

The CEO tries to use *passwordpassword*. On length alone, that passes—16 characters. Adding an uppercase letter gives her credit for one character, letting her trim the password to *passworDpasswor*. A number gives her credit for one more character, reducing it to 14: *passw0rDpassw0*. Yes, there are two digits, but the digits credit is capped at one. She can get up to three credits for non-alphanumeric characters, though. So *passw0rD!@#* is a mere 11 characters, but with the credits has a scored length of 16.

Users who create complex passwords get rewarded with shorter passwords.[24]

Common Options

These options apply whether you're defining requirements or using credits.

The *difok* option sets the minimum number of new characters in the new password. This defaults to 5. The new password must include at least five characters that don't appear in the old password. If you require long passwords, increase this.

The *maxrepeat* option sets the maximum number of times a character can be repeated in a row. The default is 0, disabling the check. Setting this to 1 disallows having the same character twice in a row.

With *maxclassrepeat*, you can limit how many characters of a particular class appear together. It's normally set to 0, disabling the check. Setting this to, say, 4, would disallow passwords containing random-looking strings like *alqkn* or *81930*, as they're longer than 4. You could use all of these characters, but you'd have to break them up with other character classes in the middle.

The *maxsequence* option sets the maximum length of an increasing or decreasing sequence, like *abcde* or *876543*. It defaults to 0, disabling this check.

If the *gecoscheck* field is set to any number other than 0, pam_pwquality compares the password to the user's `/etc/passwd` entry. Matching any word longer than three characters in `/etc/passwd` makes pam_pwquality reject the password.

---

24   I reward most of my users by reducing the voltage on the random electric shocks, but whatever works for you.

The *badwords* option can be set to a space-separated list of words forbidden to appear in passwords. If you're using this option, I highly recommend using a configuration file rather than entering the whole list in an `/etc/pam.d` file.

Finally, *enforce_for_root* tells pam_pwquality to impose restrictions even on the **root** account. Normally, **root** can assign a user's password to *password* if she pleases.

With pam_pwquality and pam_passwdqc, you can force your users to create less awful passwords. Don't expect them to thank you, though.

Afterword

PAM is a powerful tool meant to simplify systems administration, and instead it has bewildered, befuddled, and bedeviled sysadmins almost since its inception. I should know. I'm one of the folks who spent years trying to understand PAM. Every time I thought I knew what I was doing, reality gave this great big belly laugh and said, "Oh, yeah?"

Reality is kind of a jerk. But anyway…

This is my tenth self-published technical book—or, as the spine of the print edition says, number A. It's my eighteenth tech book, and my twenty-fifth book. It seems a good spot to say a couple of things that need saying.

I'm amazed, gratified, and a little humbled by the mostly positive reaction my readers have offered my work. Thanks to all of you, I'm now making a living writing books on comparatively obscure computing topics. I'm very grateful for that.

But speaking of "making a living," why would I write this book? PAM is not a hot topic like ZFS. It's not ubiquitous the way SSH is—yes, most everybody in IT passes through PAM at some point in their day, but not many people have to configure it. I wrote this book not because I thought I'd make a fortune, but because I think the systems administration community needs it.

I hope that this book saves you pain.

If not, I recommend aspirin, exercise, and doing something wholly unrelated to computers until the agony fades. Yes, that might take the rest of your life.

Sponsors

The following fine folks thought that this book was important enough that they offered me financial support as I produced it. Ebook sponsors paid at least $20 for the privilege of getting their name in the electronic version, while the people who sponsored the print edition coughed up at least $100 to get their name in actual ink.

Thanks to everyone who contributed. While I don't *need* sponsorships, they unquestionably make my life much simpler. I spent the money well, on stuff I really enjoy that's bad for me. My sincere thanks to you all.

Print Sponsors

Stefan Johnson
Hugh Brown
Wouter Clarie
Phi Network Systems
tanamar corporation

Never miss a new Lucas release!

Sign up for Michael W Lucas' mailing list.
https://www.michaelwlucas.com/mailing-lists

More Tech Books from Michael W Lucas

Absolute BSD
Absolute OpenBSD [1st and 2nd edition]
Cisco Routers for the Desperate [1st and 2nd edition]
PGP and GPG
Absolute FreeBSD
Network Flow Analysis

the IT Mastery Series

SSH Mastery
DNSSEC Mastery
Sudo Mastery
FreeBSD Mastery: Storage Essentials
Networking for Systems Administrators
Tarsnap Mastery
FreeBSD Mastery: ZFS
FreeBSD Mastery: Specialty Filesystems
FreeBSD Mastery: Advanced ZFS
PAM Mastery

Relayd & httpd Mastery (coming soon!)

www.ingramcontent.com/pod-product-compliance
Lightning Source LLC
Chambersburg PA
CBHW052142070326
40690CB00047B/1350